Myths

Robert Pierce

Betty Jane Wagner

James Moffett, *Senior Editor*

Ronald Goodman

Houghton Mifflin Company • Boston

Atlanta   Dallas   Geneva, Illinois   Hopewell, New Jersey   Palo Alto

ISBN: 0-395-13744-6

Illustrated by Victor Mojica
and Michael Gabriel

Photos by Jeff Albertson (STOCK, Boston), Lou Bernstein, George W. Gardner, Charles Gatewood, Patricia Hollander Gross (STOCK, Boston), David Haas, Michal Heron, Jay Seeley, Frank Siteman, Peter Travers, Ulrike Welsch.

Cover photos by Bonnie Unsworth

Acknowledgments

"The Origin of Death" and "The Separation of God from Man" from TALES TOLD IN TOGOLAND, by Paul Radin and James Sweeney. Reprinted by permission of Greenwood Publishers, Westport, Connecticut.

"Gilgamesh: The Story of Enkidu" adapted from GILGAMESH by Bernarda Bryson. All rights reserved. Reproduced by permission of Holt, Rinehart and Winston, Inc.

"Oedipus, King of Thebes" from MYTHS OF GREECE AND ROME by Helene Guerber. Reprinted by permission of George G. Harrap & Company, Ltd., London.

"Cupid and Psyche" from ORPHEUS: MYTHS OF THE WORLD, by Padraic Colum. Reprinted by permission of the author.

"Roll Over" from THE BEGINNING by Maria Leach, Copyright © 1956 by Funk & Wagnalls. Reprinted with permission of the publisher.

"The Story of Ra" from A BOOK OF MYTHS. Edited and retold by Roger Lancelyn Green. Illus. by Kiddell-Monroe. Children's Illustrated Classic. Published by E. P. Dutton & Co., Inc. and reprinted and recorded with their permission. Reprinted in Canada with permission of J. M. Dent & Sons Ltd.

"Hercules" from MYTHOLOGY, copyright 1942 by Edith Hamilton, copyright renewed © 1969 by Dorian Fielding Reid, copyright renewed © 1969 by Doris Fielding Reid, Executrix of the will of Edith Hamilton.

"Thor's Journey to Utgard" adapted from TALES OF THE NORSE GODS AND HEROES, by Barbara Leonie Picard. Reprinted by permission of Oxford University Press.

"Theseus" reprinted by permission from HEROES, GODS, AND MONSTERS OF THE GREEK MYTHS by Bernard Evslin, © 1966, 1967 by Scholastic Magazines, Inc.

Contents

(1) The Origin of Death   *Paul Radin and James Sweeney*
AFRICA

(5) Gilgamesh: The Story of Enkidu   *Bernarda Bryson*
BABYLONIA

(14) Oedipus, King of Thebes   *Helene Guerber*
GREECE

22 The Separation of God from Man
Paul Radin and James Sweeney
AFRICA

(24) Cupid and Psyche   *Padraic Colum*
GREECE

42 Roll Over   *Maria Leach*
AMERICAN INDIAN

(47) The Story of Ra   *Roger Lancelyn Green*
EGYPT

54 Hercules   *Edith Hamilton*
GREECE

72 Thor's Journey to Utgard   *Barbara Leonie Picard*
SCANDINAVIA

87 Theseus   *Bernard Evslin*
GREECE

107 Further Reading

Next, see "Myth Making," "Tall Tales," "A Hero or Heroine for Our Times," "Hell and Heaven," "Mod Myths and Legends," "Want Ad Puzzles," and "Picture Symbols" in MAKING THINGS UP; "Reading to Others" in PROJECTS AND PROCESSES and "Story in Disguise" and "Story Over" in ACTING OUT.

○ For a recording of this selection, see *Myths* in the LISTENING LIBRARY.

The Origin of Death

Long, long ago there was a great famine in the world and a certain young man, while wandering in search of food, strayed into a part of the bush where he had never been before. Presently he perceived a strange mass lying on the ground. He approached and saw that it was the body of a giant whose hair resembled that of white men in that it was silky rather than woolly. It was of incredible length and stretched as far as from Krachi to Salaga. The young man was properly awed at the spectacle, and wished to withdraw, but the giant, noticing him, asked what he wanted.

The young man told about the famine and begged the giant to give him some food. The latter agreed on condition that the youth would serve him for awhile. This matter having been arranged, the giant said that his name was Owuo, or Death, and he then gave the boy some meat.

Never before had the boy tasted such fine food, and he was well pleased with his bargain. He served the giant for a long time and received plenty of meat, but one day he grew home-sick, and he begged his master to give him a short holiday. The giant agreed, if the youth would promise to bring another boy in his place. So the youth returned to his village and there persuaded his brother to go with him into the bush, and he gave him to Owuo.

In course of time, the youth became hungry again and longed for the meat which Owuo had taught him to like so much. So one day he made his way back to the giant's abode. The latter asked him what he wanted, and when the youth told him that he wanted once more to taste the good meat, the giant bade him enter the hut and take as much as he liked, but added that he would have to work for him again.

The youth agreed and entered the hut. He ate as much as he could and went to work at the task which his master set him. The work continued for a long time and the boy ate his fill every day. But, to his surprise, he never saw anything of his brother, and, whenever he asked about him, the giant told him that the lad was away on business.

Once more the youth grew homesick and asked for leave to return to his village. The giant agreed on condition that he would bring a girl for him, Owuo, to wed. So the youth went home and there persuaded his sister to go into the bush and marry the giant. The girl agreed, and took with her a slave companion, and they all repaired to the giant's abode. There the youth left the two girls and went back to the village.

It was not very long after that he again grew hungry and longed for a taste of the meat. So he made his way once more into the bush and found the giant. The giant did not seem overpleased to see the boy and grumbled at being bothered a third time. However, he told the boy to go into the inner chamber of his hut and take what he wanted. The youth did so and took up a bone which he began to devour. To his horror he recognized it at once as being the bone of his sister. He looked around at all the rest of the meat and saw that it was that of his sister and her slave girl.

Thoroughly frightened, he escaped from the house and ran back to the village. There he told the elders what he had done and the awful thing he had seen. At once the alarm was sounded and all the people went out into the bush to see for themselves the dreadful thing they had heard about. When they drew near to the giant they grew afraid at the sight of so evil a monster. They went back to the village and consulted among themselves what they had best do. At last it was agreed to go to Salaga where the end of the giant's hair was, and set a light to it. This was done and when the hair was burning well they returned to the bush and watched the giant.

Presently the giant began to toss about and to sweat. It was quite evident that he was beginning to feel the heat. The nearer the flames advanced, the more he tossed and grumbled. At last the flames reached his head and for the moment the giant was dead.

The villagers approached him cautiously, and the young

man noticed magic powder which had been concealed in the roots of the giant's hair. He took it and called the others to come and see what he had found. No one could say what power this medicine might have, but an old man suggested that no harm would be done if they sprinkled some of it on the bones and the meat in the hut. This idea was carried out, and to the surprise of everyone the girls and the boy at once returned to life.

The youth, who still had some of the powder left, proposed to put it on the giant, but at this there was great uproar as the people feared Owuo might come to life again. The boy, therefore, by way of compromise, sprinkled it into the eye of the dead giant. At once the eye opened and the people fled in terror. But alas, it is from that eye that death comes, for every time that Owuo shuts that eye a man dies, and unfortunately, he is forever blinking and winking.

Gilgamesh:
The Story of Enkidu

The epic of Gilgamesh is one of man's earliest stories. What follows is that part of the epic that tells of primeval man — Enkidu — and how he came to be civilized.

I. *The Coming of Enkidu*

The world of Gilgamesh was hemmed in by the mighty mountains of Mashu that were the edge between day and night. It was circled by the Bitter River that flowed round and round it unceasingly, and that had no beginning and no end. No one knew what lay beyond the river, since the very touch of its waters was death. Some speculated that to the north of it lay the mountains-without-end and to the south, the sea-without-end, but still no one was sure.

To the west was the void into which the sun set. There opened those rocky caverns through which the sun passed under the earth and back into the Eastern Garden where his home was and whence he arose again in the mornings. So much was known.

Now Gilgamesh was king of this land. He had built many towering walls to protect his city, Uruk, from all sorts of evil — armies of enemy kings, floods, wild beasts, and unfriendly gods. The elders of the city did not like the walls and decided they would ask the gods to punish Gilgamesh for building them. They prayed to the gods to create a wild beast of a man to come and challenge Gilgamesh. The gods finally agreed, and Aruru, she who was responsible for the shaping of human forms, reached down to the earth and scooped up a huge lump of clay.

This she began to model and shape, spitting on it from time to time in order to keep it soft and malleable.

Aruru made the clay into the form of a man, one so like Gilgamesh that he could have been his brother. But this man

(5)

was unkempt and savage in his looks, and from his head there arose two majestic horns like those of some wild beast.

Aruru then carried him in her arms into the depths of a cedar forest and laid him on the earth. This was Enkidu.

He slept there on the earth for some time and then wakened and looked around him. He didn't know who he was or where he had come from.

But one thing was certain: that he was hungry. He walked for some time and at length came upon a fig tree with ripe figs lying on the ground below. He ate some and found them good. He next ate a green sprig of cedar, but that he didn't like and he spit it out. He returned to the fig tree and ate more of the fruit together with the stems, worms, and a few leaves.

He wandered about in the sun-spotted forest and found a spring bubbling with cool water. He dipped his hands into it; he drank; he rolled in it; Enkidu was beginning to enjoy his newly given life.

He squatted on his haunches beside the pool, listening to its sounds, watching its sparkling lights. A rabbit crept to its edge to drink and Enkidu leaped away terrified. But since the creature also fled, he returned to his place. And when another rabbit came he was no longer afraid. He watched a wild pig drink, a fox, a jackal.

Birds came to the spring and dipped their wings in it, drank, and fluttered their feathers. A small wild horse came to drink, and then a gazelle. Enkidu so admired this gentle-eyed creature that he reached out to touch it. It shivered and crouched to run, but then hesitated and stood still. The gazelle became Enkidu's first friend, and from it he learned to eat grass and the petals of flowers.

The pool became his living-place. He stared at the animals, touched them, tamed them one by one. He found that he could run and leap with the gazelle, but he could not fly with the birds however much he tried.

One evening a lion, breathing heavily, came near the pool. The other animals fled but Enkidu stood still watching the huge beast.

Suddenly its yellow eyes looked at him, and before he could run the beast had leaped on him. He felt its terrible claws rip into the flesh along his sides. Enkidu cried out with pain.

But then he wrestled with this animal, his first enemy. He first felt anger and the mighty strength of his muscles. He bent the lion backward, he twisted its neck. They fell to the ground each trying to kill the other. Enkidu grasped the neck and the back leg of the beast; he wrenched its back and saw the great creature lie writhing and roaring on the earth. There was foam around its mouth; the tongue rolled sidewise and hung piteously out of the beast's mouth. Enkidu knew that it was thirsty; he felt pity and he carried water in his hands to slake the animal's thirst. Then he washed away the blood from its wounds, caressed its mane and watched over it through the night. In the morning the lion limped away, but it returned again and again, and it too became Enkidu's friend.

11. *The Luring of Enkidu*

A young hunter ran into the hut of his father, a shepherd, and hid himself in a corner.

"What's wrong with you?" his father shouted. "Why do you behave like that?"

The hunter opened his mouth and cried out, "O father, there is a strange man I've seen in the forest and wandering over the steppes. How many times have I complained to you that my traps were broken and robbed! Well, today I saw the thief — a terrifying sight, father, a man whose strength is like that of the hosts of heaven! He filled the pits that I had dug. He broke open my traps. He freed the animals; he carried them off as a mother lion might carry off her whelps!"[1]

"Come, come!" said the shepherd. "You're seeing things, son! The game is scarce; you've been careless with your traps!"

"The hair springs out of his head like a field of grain, and he has the horns of a wild beast!"

"If he stole your catch of game, my son, why didn't you stop him?"

"He is taller and more powerful than Gilgamesh the King. I was numbed with fear!"

"If what you say is true, son, then we must report the matter to the King. But if you have lied, we will be in disgrace forever!"

---

[1] *whelps:* pups

The shepherd and his son went into the city of Uruk to make their complaint. But there the populace were already spreading rumors about the wild man. Some said, "He is covered with hair from head to foot," and others, "He is taller than a giant and eats grass with the gazelles!"

It was the eldest of the elders who led the hunter and his father before the King. "O Gilgamesh," said the elder, "there is a wild man that terrorizes the countryside. He robs the hunter of his game and disperses the herds of the shepherd. He turns all who see him numb with fear — indeed I've heard that he is taller and more powerful than Gilgamesh the King!"

Gilgamesh, who feared nothing, might have been expected to say, "Then it's I who will go out and subdue him and bring him captive to the city!" Not at all; he sent to the temple of Ishtar for a certain priestess, one called Harim, servant of the goddess.

He said to her, "Harim, I have a certain task for you; it is one that turns the boldest hunters numb with fear!"

"Then I am afraid," said Harim.

The eldest of the elders spoke angrily, "This is not a girl's task, O King; it is a task for a brave man — a hero!"

"Tut tut," said Gilgamesh. "It is a girl's task of smiles and charm. Go, Harim; soften the heart of the wild man and bring him back to the city!"

Harim was led by the hunter to the edge of the forest, and she noted that he began to tremble with fear. "Go back to the hut of your father," she commanded. "If I can tame the wild man, I will lead him into the city alone."

The hunter was shamed by the girl's bravery. "Do not enter the forest, O Harim; I myself will go." But the priestess laughed at him and sent him home.

She went among the dark cedars; she listened to the sounds of birds and of monkeys chattering. She noted the bits of sunlight that filtered through the branches and lit up flowers, moss, and bracken on the forest floor. "How peaceful a place this is! How could any evil thing lurk here?" Harim found a fresh spring bubbling with cool water. She sat beside it on a stone, untied her sandals, and dipped her feet in the water.

Enkidu came to the place with the small wild horse and the gazelle. As they drew near, the two beasts became nervous, sniffed the air, and fled. But Enkidu stood still; he wondered what new danger was near, what unknown beast might have come to the water.

When he saw the girl sitting there his breath failed and he was overcome. He had not yet seen a human being, and this creature seemed to him the most admirable, the most enchanting being that he had ever seen. He stood quietly in order not to frighten her.

Harim gazed at his giant figure, his soaring horns, and his unkempt looks and would have run away, but she could not move. She opened her mouth to scream and could not make a sound. She was numb with terror. And Enkidu noting this remained quiet; he had made friends with many timid creatures and he knew their ways.

When the priestess saw the gentleness of his manner, her courage returned to her somewhat. She called out shyly, "Hello!"

Enkidu knew no words. He could babble somewhat as the monkeys did. He could bark quite like a fox, or trill like many birds. He had various calls of greeting for his wild friends, but this new animal made sounds that he could not understand.

He neither barked nor roared, but stood perplexed looking at the girl. Again she spoke, and now held out her hands to him in greeting.

Enkidu approached slowly and sat on the earth beside the white feet of Harim. She said all sorts of things to him and he understood nothing. She asked him many questions and he could not reply. But he felt ecstasy in his heart, and great contentment in merely sitting beside her.

How easy was her conquest of Enkidu! Harim smiled, but she now began to feel a new sort of fear. How could she lead this great fellow, so gentle and so innocent, back to the city of Uruk? Would the people set on him and kill him? Would they jeer at him? Would the King have him put into a cage and carried through the streets on the backs of soldiers? She shuddered.

No, first she must teach him the ways of people, the conformity of life.

"*Al-ka ti-ba i-na ga-ag-ga-ri!*" said Harim. "Come, rise from the ground!" But the wild man did not understand. Thus, she taught him the word for standing, and then after that, the word for sitting. She taught him the words for walking, running, talking, laughing, eating, and he repeated each one, learning it. She taught him the words for trees and for stones and for water, for earth and for the trailing vines that grew beside the spring, and for the spring itself. She taught him the words for feet and hands and the names of all the fingers and all the myriad words of love.

Thus patiently, Harim taught Enkidu to be like ordinary men. She cut his hair and combed it in the way of people of the city. She made him bathe; she tore her long tunic into two parts, making of one half a garment for Enkidu, keeping the other half for herself.

Again she spoke to him, and now he understood, "*A-na-tal-ka En-ki-du ki-ma ili ta-ba-as-si!*" — "I gaze upon you, Enkidu; you are like a god!"

He brought her gifts — all the things that he had come to know and love in the forest and from the open steppes; wild cucumbers and cassia melon, grapes and figs and caper buds from the dry rocks. He brought her blossoms of golden mimosa

and fragrant branches of jasmine.

After some time had passed Harim said, "Now I will lead Enkidu out among the people and everyone will admire him!" But still she feared for his life so she took him first to the hut of the shepherd.

At the edge of the forest Enkidu stopped and turned back. He was overcome with regret; how could he leave forever his friends of the woods and wild places? Who would protect them? Who would release them from the traps? How could he leave behind his friend the little wild horse, or the gazelle, the rabbits, the monkeys that had taught him to play games?

But as he approached they leaped away startled. The rabbit hid trembling in the grass and the birds took off with a wild flutter of wings.

Enkidu threw himself to the ground, weeping. "O Harim, what have I done? How have I made all my friends into strangers? Why do they run from me?

"Enkidu is no longer a wild creature. He is no longer a beast of the forest and the open plain. Enkidu is now a man. He will live among men and be eminent among men!"

Enkidu followed regretfully as the priestess led him toward the hut of the shepherd. This man greeted him with awe and admiration, but his son fled from the place and hid in the sheepfold. After some time he returned, running. "Father, a lion has entered the fold! It is devouring the lambs!"

Enkidu went to the sheepfold where again he wrestled with the lion, his friend who no longer knew him. Again he overcame the beast, but he let it go free. He lifted the lambs gently, washing and tending the ones that bled. To his great joy they did not shun him or run away. Neither did the young calves nor the barnyard fowl. A dog followed him wagging its tail. A cat smoothed its fur against his legs, and again he was content.

In the hut of the shepherd Enkidu learned to sit on a chair and to wash his hands before eating. He learned how to care for animals, to make plants grow, and to build with mud and brick and reeds. He learned to play on a flute. He ate bread. There he tasted the strong sesame wine and drank seven cups. His face shone, he rejoiced; he sang.

Harim smiled. "Now Enkidu has become like a man, we shall go into the city!"

Oedipus, King of Thebes

as told by Helene Guerber

GREECE

There was a curse upon the family of Laius, King of Thebes, and the story of his unhappy son Oedipus is the story of the fulfilling of that curse. Laius, driven from his kingdom, took refuge with Pelops, son of Tantalus, and then most ungratefully kidnaped the boy Chrysippus, son of his protector. In course of time Laius recovered his kingdom, and married a princess called Jocasta, but Apollo warned him that owing to his graceless conduct towards Pelops there was a dark curse on him and his, and that his own son would slay him.

When a boy was born to Jocasta the King called an aged shepherd to him and bade him carry the babe to a lonely hilltop called Mount Cithaeron, first piercing his feet so that he should die. But the forlorn little creature was found and carried to the palace of King Polybus of Corinth, whose Queen, Merope, having no child of her own, resolved to adopt the foundling, to whom she gave the name of Oedipus — "swollen-footed."

The boy grew up believing himself to be the true-born son of the royal pair, and all went well until one day a drunken reveller[1] taunted him with being nothing of the sort. In order to learn the truth the young prince consulted the famous oracle at Delphi, which, without giving him a definite answer to his question, told him that it was his destiny to slay his father, marry his mother, and bring sorrow on his native city.

Thinking that this terrible decree referred to Polybus and Merope, Oedipus fled from Corinth, resolved never to return. It happened that his lonely journey took him to a point where two roads met, and there he encountered another traveller, an old man in a chariot, escorted by servants and preceded by a herald.[2] Oedipus, who was accustomed to being treated with

[1] *reveller:* merry-maker
[2] *herald:* announcer

great deference,[3] refused to pull his own chariot aside when curtly ordered to do so by the herald, who thereupon killed one of his horses. Furious, Oedipus leaped forth, and in the struggle which followed he slew the old man and all the attendants except one.

Nobody who is acquainted with the dreary infallibility[4] of Greek oracles will need to be told that the old man was Laius, King of Thebes.

Oedipus and the Sphinx

Oedipus, little recking that one part of the curse had been fulfilled, pursued his journey and at last reached the city of Thebes, his own native city, though he knew it not. There he found great dismay and confusion on all sides. The realm was being ravaged by a dread Sphinx, a monster with the head and shoulders of a woman and the body of a lioness, who crouched on a rock, and asked riddles of every traveller who passed. Nobody guessed the right answer, and everybody who failed to do so became the Sphinx's prey. Oedipus, careless of a life which he had ceased to prize, approached the monster, and expressed his willingness to try his fortune. "What animal is it," asked the Sphinx, "which in the morning goes on four feet, at noon on two, and in the evening on three?" "That animal," answered Oedipus promptly, "is a man. As a child he crawls, as a man he walks erect, in his old age he supports himself on a staff." This was the correct answer; and the Sphinx, furious at having found some one who could guess it, flung herself from the rock and died.

News meanwhile had reached the Thebans of the mysterious death of their absent King, but there was nothing to connect that event with the coming of the youth who had freed them from the horror at their gates. Creon, Queen Jocasta's brother, who was acting as regent, offered the crown, together with Jocasta's hand in marriage, to the astonished Oedipus, who accepted both, and who reigned in peace and prosperity for some years.

Oedipus Rex

Four children were born to Oedipus the King and his Queen — two sons, Eteocles and Polynices, and two daughters, Ismene and

[3] *deference:* respect
[4] *infallibility:* unfailingness

Antigone. It seemed as if all was well with the royal line of Thebes. And then plague and famine descended upon the land, and the people gathered in great multitudes outside the palace doors, imploring their King to intercede for them with the gods who were apparently upset. Creon, the Queen's brother, was sent to Delphi to find what might be done to lift this blight from Thebes, and he returned with the puzzling message that an unclean thing, dwelling in that realm, must be cast out, and that the murderer of the dead King Laius must be tracked and punished.

It is certainly rather curious that Oedipus should not have made close inquiry into the circumstances surrounding the death of his predecessor, but he now threw himself eagerly into the task. Where, he asked, had the old King died? Did no one bring some tidings of the manner of his murder? Creon answered that Laius had been set upon by robbers and slain when he was on the road to Delphi, and that only one of those who went with him had returned, bemused [5] with terror. In the confusion caused by the Sphinx and her ravages no man had at that time taken thought to avenge the King. "Then," said Oedipus, "be it my charge so to do. And solemnly I curse the murderer of Laius."

In those days lived a blind seer called Tiresias, and of him Oedipus resolved to seek counsel. To his surprise the old man was strangely reluctant to speak what was in his mind, though the King knelt before him, with upraised hands, saying, "Lo! We all bow down, imploring thine aid." Finding that prayers were of no avail, Oedipus grew angry, and it was then that Tiresias turned upon him with the terrible words, "Thou art thyself this unclean thing that must be driven forth." In his astonishment the King imagined that his brother-in-law, Creon, was plotting against him with the aid of the sightless seer,[6] but Tiresias rebuked him sternly for the thought, and asked him how it befell that he knew nothing of his own birth. When Oedipus, stung by fear, grew angry again the old man sobered him with the words, "The two who gave thee birth held me in honor."

"You speak in dark riddles," said the King, and Tiresias answered tauntingly, "Aye, you too were a reader of riddles once. But now I tell you that the man you seek, the unclean murderer, is here."

[5] *bemused:* stunned
[6] *seer:* person gifted with special vision, often into the future

Still obsessed by the unjust thought that all this was part of a dark scheme of Creon to drive him from the throne, Oedipus uttered the doom of death against his brother-in-law. But Jocasta, the Queen, came forth from the brazen doors of the palace, and demanded to know the cause of the clash between the two men. "Creon says," declared Oedipus, "that I am the murderer of Laius." Of course Creon had said no such thing, and when he denied it the King retorted, "This evil seer of thine says it was thus."

Jocasta, convinced of her brother's innocence, and anxious to soothe the King's fury, then said, "What talk is this of seers? No mortal man may read the purposes of the high gods. Hearken unto me. An oracle once said that my husband Laius should be slain by a son of mine, but when I bore my lord a son the babe was laid upon Mount Cithaeron to die. And so the oracle was proved false. For Laius was killed by robbers, not by the hand of my child, long since dead."

Terror-smitten, the unhappy Oedipus poured forth stammering questions, scarcely daring to listen to the replies. Where exactly was Laius slain? At the crossroads, in the land of Phocis, where one road comes from Daulia and one from Delphi. How long ago? As many years and months ago as the coming of Oedipus to Thebes. What manner of man was the old King? Tall, with white hair; in figure much like Oedipus himself. How many men went with him? Four, of whom one was a herald. Where is the one man who escaped alive? "On the day that you were crowned king," answered the Queen, "that man prayed that he might be sent to some place in the mountains, to tend his sheep, far from Thebes."

Then, the terrible truth breaking on him only by degrees, Oedipus realized that the curse he had uttered upon the slayer of Laius had been called down upon his own head. But he clung to one shred of hope. He must speak with the herdsman. If the fellow stuck to his tale of a band of robbers having assailed the King all would be well. But if instead he confessed that the slayer was one solitary man there could be no further doubt or uncertainty. So messengers were sent to fetch the herdsman, and in the interval a herald came from Corinth saying that Polybus was dead, and that the Corinthians called Oedipus to come and be their King. Again Jocasta spoke tauntingly of oracles. "Look," she said to Oedipus, "you have lived in exile all these years because Apollo foretold that you would kill your father — and the old man has died in peace, not by your hand." "May be," returned the King, "but Merope still lives, and while she lives I cannot return to Corinth."

The herald, hearing these words, could not conceal his bewilderment, and Oedipus had no choice but to tell him the story of the oracle, and of his flight from Corinth and his exile in Thebes. "Hearken, my lord the king," said the herald then, "I can free you from this fear. You were no son of Polybus and Merope. None was born to them. It was I who carried you to the palace in my arms." "Am I then *your* son?" asked the King. "No more than you were his. I was tending sheep on Mount Cithaeron one day, and another shepherd drew near with a weeping child in his arms — a child with a cruel iron spike driven through its feet. This man bade me take the babe and bear it to some far place to die. But I had pity on it, and, thinking there might be some mystery about its birth, I bore it to the palace of my King."

"Who was this shepherd?" asked Oedipus.

"One of those," returned the messenger, "who tended the flocks of Laius, King of Thebes."

His heart cold within him, Oedipus gave orders that the man should be sought, and very soon it became clear that it was the same who had escaped from the struggle at the crossroads, and who had asked to be sent to some far place on the day that Oedipus had been crowned.

When the old shepherd was found and brought before the King all doubt was soon at an end. He and the herald recognized each other. And, timidly and reluctantly answering the breathless questions of Oedipus, he acknowledged that it was from Jocasta's own arms that he had received the child whom afterwards, thinking maybe to save its life, he had given to another herdsman met by chance on Mount Cithaeron.

The King fled into the palace with a cry of anguish, but the unhappy man's cup of sorrow was not yet full. In the inner room he found Jocasta lying dead, slain by her own hand. From her mantle[7] he snatched the broad brooch[8] of gold, and

---

[7] *mantle:* cloak

[8] *brooch:* a clasp with pin

with it he wounded his own eyes, so that never more should he behold the light of day.

The doom[9] spoken by the oracle had now been fulfilled. It remained only to release the people of Thebes from plague and famine by driving forth from their midst the unwitting murderer and criminal whom they had honored for many years as a just and goodly king. Oedipus pronounced the sentence on himself, and declared that he would make his way to the wild and solitary hill of Cithaeron, the place where his father and mother had willed that he should die.

[9] *doom:* prophecy

The Separation of God from Man

In the beginning of days, Wulbari[1] and man lived close together and Wulbari lay on top of Mother Earth, Asase Ya. Thus it happened that, as there was so little space to move about in, man annoyed the divinity, who in disgust went away and rose up to the present place where one can admire him but not reach him.

He was annoyed for a number of reasons. An old woman, while making her fufu[2] outside her hut, kept on knocking Wulbari with her pestle. This hurt him and, as she persisted, he was forced to go higher out of her reach. Besides the smoke of the cooking fires got into his eyes so that he had to go farther away. According to others, however, Wulbari, being so close to men, made a convenient sort of towel, and the people used to wipe their dirty fingers on him. This naturally annoyed him. Yet this was not so bad a grievance as that which caused We, the Wulbari of the Kassena people, to remove himself out of the reach of men. He did so because an old woman, anxious to make soup, used to cut off a bit of him at each mealtime, and We, being pained at this treatment, went higher.

[1] *Wulbari:* God
[2] *fufu:* mush

22

Cupid and Psyche

as told by Padriac Colum

In a far country there was a king and queen who had three daughters: each of the maidens was beautiful; the youngest of them, however, had such shape and lineaments[1] that all words said in praise of beauty seemed but poor and empty when used about hers. Men came to where she dwelt as to a shrine; they would kiss the tips of their right hands at the sight of her, thus paying to this maiden (Psyche she was named) the same homage that was paid to Venus, the immortal Goddess.

Indeed, it began to be said that Venus had forsaken the courts of Heaven, and had come down to earth as a mortal maiden, and dwelt amongst men in the person of the youngest daughter of the king and queen of that far country. Then men sailed no longer to where there were the famous shrines of the Goddess Venus. The shrines in Paphos, and Cnidus, and Cythera were forsaken of worshipers, and men paid their devotions to a mortal maiden, to Psyche. When she went forth from her father's house in the morning the folk strewed flowers along the way, and sacrifices that should have been made to no one but to the immortal Goddess were made to her.

The rumors of such happenings soon reached to Venus herself. She said, "Shall I, judged the fairest amongst the immortal Goddesses by the Shepherd of Ida, shall I have mine honors taken away from me by an earthly girl? Not so. Little joy shall this Psyche have of the loveliness that the vain imaginations of the crowd have bestowed upon her." Thereupon Venus called to her son. She brought him with her to that far country, and she showed him the maiden Psyche as she walked the ways of the city. "I pray thee," she said, "to let thy mother have a vengeance

[1] *lineaments:* features

24

that it is fitting she should have. See to it that this girl becomes the slave of an unworthy love." She embraced him and she left him there, and she sailed for whatever shrine of hers had still some worshipers.

Her son was Cupid, that winged boy who goes through men's houses by night, armed with his bow and arrow, troubling their wedded lives. She left him there, gazing on the maiden Psyche. And gazing upon her, Cupid fell deeply in love with the maiden. He had no mind to carry out the command of his mother; he did not want to smite her mind with the madness of an unworthy love; rather he thought upon how he might win for himself the one who was fairer than any being upon earth or even in the heaven above.

And Psyche, adored by all for her beauty, had no joy in the fruit of it. She knew that she was wondered at, but wondered at as the work of the craftsman is wondered at that has in it some likeness of divinity[2]. No man sought her in marriage. Her sisters were wedded, but she came to their age and passed their age and remained unasked for. She sat at home, and in her heart she cursed the beauty that pleased all men while it set her apart from the close thought of all. At last the king, her father, was forced to send and inquire of an oracle what he should do with this daughter of his. An answer came that meant a dreadful doom. "Let the maiden be placed on the top of a certain mountain, adorned as for marriage and for death. Look not for a son-in-law of mortal birth; he who will take her to his side is the serpent whom even the Gods are in dread of, and who makes the bodiless ones on the Styx[3] afraid."

For many days after this doom had been made known there were lamentations in the king's household. Then, at last, knowing that the doom told might not be avoided, the queen brought out the adornments for her daughter's marriage and gathered a company to conduct the maiden to her dread bridal. All was made ready. But the torch lighted for the wedding gathered ashes and made a dark smoke; the joyful sound of the pipe changed into a wail; underneath her yellow wedding-veil the bride trembled and wept. The ceremonies for the marriage having been accomplished

[2] *divinity:* Godliness
[3] *Styx:* the river of Hades, Hell

with hearts bowed down as at a funeral, Psyche was led from the city and to the place appointed on the mountain-top.

As she went she said to those who were with her, "This is the fruit of my much-talked-of loveliness! Ye weep for me now, but when the folk celebrated me with divine honors — then was the time you should have wept for me as for one already dead! The name and titles given me have been my destruction! Lead me on and set my feet upon the appointed place! I am impatient to behold my bridegroom and give myself up to the serpent whom even the Gods are fearful of."

Then she said to her father and mother, "Do not waste what life you have weeping over me." She bade them good-bye. They left her on the mountaintop and went back mournfully to the city. Then night came down upon them there; they shut themselves in their house and gave themselves up to perpetual night.

As for Psyche, she stood upon the mountaintop in fear and trembling. The breeze came, the gentle Zephyrus. Zephyrus lifted Psyche up; he bore her, her bridal vesture floating on either side, down the side of the mountain, and he set her lightly amidst the flowers of the valley below.

Lightly was it all done. Psyche lay on a dewy bed in the valley, resting from the tumult of the days that had gone by. She awoke. She saw a grove with a fountain of water that was as clear as glass in the midst of it, and, by the fountain, a dwelling place.

Psyche thought that this dwelling place must be the abode of one of the immortal Gods. Golden pillars held up the roof. Cedar wood and ivory formed the arches. The walls were latticed with silver. Before the house, creatures of the wood and wild — rabbits, and squirrels, and deer sported, and all the birds that Psyche had ever seen or heard sang in the trees. And the very path that led to the house was set in stones that made pictures and stories.

Upon this path she went. She crossed the threshold of the house and went within. Beautiful things were there, and no locks, no chains, no guardian protected them. As she went through the house, drawn on by more and more delight, she heard a voice that said, "Lady and mistress! All that is here is thine! Rest now and relieve thy weariness. We whose voices thou hearest are servants to thee; when thou wilt, a feast fit for a queen will be made ready for thee."

Psyche went to sleep knowing that some divine being had care for her. She awoke and went to the bath; thereafter she sat down to the food that had been made ready for her — a banquet, indeed! Still she saw no one. She heard voices, but those who served her remained invisible. When the feast was ended one whom she saw not entered and sang for her — sang to the chords of a harp that was played for her by one unseen. The night came and the lamps were lighted by unseen hands. Then they were quenched by unseen hands, and to Psyche, lying in her bed, the bridgegroom came. He departed before the dawn, and she was a wife.

The day was before her, and the attendant minstrels sang to her; she heard their voices and she heard the music they made for her. The night came; the lamps were lighted and quenched, and to Psyche her husband came as before. And as before, he departed before the dawn came. And this went on for many nights. Then to his bride one night the bridegroom said, "O Psyche, my life and my spouse! Fortune is becoming ill-favored towards us! Thou art threatened with a danger that may be mortal. Harken! Thy sisters are about to go seeking for traces of thee. They will come to the mountaintop in their search. But if their cries come to thee in this abode, do not answer, nor go forth at all. If thou dost, it may be that thou shalt bring sorrow and destruction upon us both. But that shall be as thou wilt!"

Psyche promised that she would do all he would have her do. The bridegroom departed, going forth ere the darkness had gone. That day Psyche heard the voices of her sisters as they went calling her name. And in that house empty of all save voices, she thought that she was indeed dead and cut off from her sisters and her parents. She thought upon how they had wept for her, and she wept herself to think that she had no power to console them. In the night the bridegroom returned. Kissing her face, he found it wet with tears.

He blamed her; she wept the more. Then, as dawn came, he said, "Be it as thou wilt. Let thy pain cease, and do as thou dost desire. Yet wilt thou, Psyche, remember the warning I have given thee." All this he said when she told him that she would die unless she might see and speak with her sisters who were seeking for her.

"Yet one thing shall I say to thee," he said. "If they come here to thee give them all the gifts thou wilt; but do not yield thyself to their doubts about me. Thou knowest me, thy husband. Do not yield to the counsel of thy sisters and inquire concerning my bodily form. If thou dost, thou and I may never again embrace each other."

Then Psyche wept; she said she would die a hundred times rather than forego his dear embraces. In a while he relented, and he spoke less harshly. Then Psyche said, "For the sake of the love I have given thee bid thy servant Zephyrus bring hither my sisters as he brought me." Her husband promised that this would be done. Then, ere the light appeared, he vanished.

I I

Her sisters, coming to the place where Psyche was left, sought for traces of her. Finding none they wept, lifting up their voices. Zephyrus came; he raised them up; he bore them down from that mountaintop. He bore them to the lawn that was before the house where Psyche had her abode.

She heard their cries; she came out of her wondrous house

and she brought them within it. "Enter now," she said, "and relieve your sorrow in the company of Psyche, your sister." She displayed to them all the treasures of that wondrous house; they heard the voices and they saw how the unseen ones ministered to Psyche. Her sisters were filled with wonder; but soon their wonder gave place to envy. "Who is he?" they asked, "your husband and the lord of all these wondrous things?" "A young man," said Psyche. "I would have you look upon him, but for the most part of the day he hunts upon the mountain." Then, lest the secret should slip from her tongue, she loaded her sisters with gold and gems, and, summoning Zephyrus with words that she had heard her husband utter, she commanded him to bear them to the mountaintop.

They returned to their homes, each of them filled with envy of Psyche's fortune. "Look now," they said to each other, "what has come about! We the elder sisters have been given in marriage to men we did not know and who were of little account. And she, our youngest sister, is possessed of such great riches that she is able to give us these golden things and these gems as if they were mere keepsakes. What a hoard of wealth is in her house!

You saw, sisters, the crowns, and glittering gems, and gold trodden under foot! If her husband is noble and handsome enough to match that house, then no woman in the world is as lucky or as happy as that Psyche whom we left upon the mountaintop!" And, saying this, they became more and more filled with envy, and with the malice that comes from envy unchecked.

Then one said to the other, "This husband of hers may be of divine nature, and through his mere fondness for her, he may make her a Goddess. Yes, as a Goddess she ever bore herself! How intolerable it would be if all that was thought about her were realized, and she became as one of the Immortals."

And so, filled with their envy and malice, they returned to that golden house and they said to Psyche, "Thou livest in folly, and knowst nothing of a danger that threatens thee. Thou hast never seen thy husband — that we know. But others have seen him, and they know him for a deadly serpent. Remember the words of the oracle, which declared thee destined for a devouring beast. There are those who have seen that beast at nightfall, coming back from his feeding and entering this house. And now thou art to be a mother! The beast only waits for the babe to be born so that he may devour both the babe and thee. Nothing can be done for thee, perhaps, because thou mayst delight in this rich and secret place, and even in a loathsome love. But at least we, thy sisters, have done our part in bidding thee beware!" So they spoke, and Psyche was carried away by their words, and lost the memory of her husband's commands and her own promises. She cried out in anguish, "It may be that those who say these things tell the truth! For in very truth I have never seen the face of my husband, nor know I at all what form and likeness he has. He frightens me from the sight of him, telling me that some great evil should befall if I looked upon his face. O ye who were reared with me, help, if you can, your sister, in the great peril that faces her now!"

Her sisters, filled with malice, answered, "The way to safety we have well considered, and we will show it to thee. Take a sharp knife and hide it in that part of the couch where thou art wont to lie. Place a lighted lamp behind a curtain. And when thou hearest him breathe in sleep, slip from the couch, and, holding the lamp, look upon him. Have in thy hand the knife. Then it is for thee to put forth all thy strength and strike his serpent's

30

head off. Then thou wilt be delivered from the doom which the vain talk about thy beauty brought upon thee, and thou mayst return to thy father's house."

Saying this, her sisters departed hastily. And Psyche, left alone, was tossed up and down as on the waves of the sea. The apprehension of a great calamity was upon her: she thought she could avert it by making strong her will for the deed that her sisters had counselled her to carry out. Evening came, and in haste she made ready for the terrible deed. Darkness came; he whom she had known for her bridegroom came to her out of the darkness. In a while she, lying rigidly there, knew by his breath that he was asleep.

She arose, she who before was of no strength at all; she drew forth the knife in the darkness and held it in her right hand. She took up the lighted lamp. And then she saw what lay on the couch. Then indeed she became afraid; her limbs failed under her, and she would have buried the knife in her own bosom. For there lay Love himself, with golden locks, and ruddy cheeks, and white throat. There lay Love with his pinions,[4] yet fresh with dew, spotless upon his shoulders. Smooth he was, and touched with a light that was from Venus, his mother. And at the foot of the couch his bow and arrows were laid.

Then Psyche, with indrawn breath, bent over to kiss his lips. And it chanced that a drop of burning oil from that lamp which she held fell upon his shoulder. At the touch of that burning drop, the God started up. He saw her bending over him; he saw the whole of her faithlessness; putting her hands away he lifted himself from the couch and fled away.

And Psyche, as he rose upon the wing, laid hold on him with her hands, striving to stay his flight. But she could not stay it; he went from her and she sank down upon the ground. As she lay there the dawn came, and she saw through the casement her divine lover where he rested upon a cypress tree that grew near. She could not cry out to him. He spoke to her in great emotion. "Foolish one," he said, "Venus, my mother, would have devoted thee to a love that was all baseness. Unmindful of her command I would not have that doom befall thee. Mine own flesh I pierced with mine arrow, and I took thee for my love. I brought thee here, I made thee my wife, and all only that I might seem a

[4] *pinions:* wings

monster beside thee, and that thou shouldst seek to wound the head wherein lay the eyes that were so full of love for thee. I thought I could put thee on thy guard against those who were ready to make snares for thee. Now all is over. I would but punish thee by my flight hence!"

Prostrate[5] upon the earth Psyche watched, as far as sight might reach, the flight of her spouse. When the breadth of space had parted him wholly from her, she ran without. Far she wandered from that golden house where she had dwelt with Love. She came to where a river ran. In her despair she cast herself into it. But as it happened, Pan, the rustic[6] God, was on the river bank, playing upon a reed. Hard by, his flock of goats browsed at will. The shaggy God took Psyche out of the stream. "I am but a herdsman," he said to her, "a herdsman and rustic. But I am wise by reason of my length of days and my long experience of the world. I guess by thy sorrowful eyes and thy continual sighing that thy trouble comes from love. Then, pretty maiden, listen to me, and seek not death again in the stream or elsewhere. Put aside thy woe, and make thy prayers to Cupid. He is a God who is won by service; give him, therefore, thy service."

Psyche was not able to answer anything. She left the God with his goats and went on her way. And now she was resolved to go through the world in search of Cupid, her spouse. And he, even then, was in his mother's house: he lay there in pain from the wound that the burning drop from Psyche's lamp had given him. Heart-sick was he, too. The white bird that floats over the waves and is his mother's, seeing him come back, went across the sea, and, approaching Venus as she bathed, made known to her that her son lay afflicted with some grievous hurt. Thereupon she issued from the sea, and, returning to her golden house, found Cupid there, wounded and afflicted in his mind. Soon she found out the cause of his suffering and became filled with anger. "Well done!" she cried. "To trample on thy mother's precepts[7] and to spare her enemy the cross that she had designed for her — the cross of an unworthy love! Nay, to have united yourself with her, giving me a daughter-in-law who hates me! But I will make her and thee repent of the love that has been between you, and the

---

[5] *prostrate:* stretched out face down
[6] *rustic:* rural
[7] *precepts:* principles and teachings

savor of your marriage bitter!" And saying this, Venus hastened in anger from her house.

III

Psyche was wandering hither and thither, seeking her husband, her whole heart set upon soothing his anger by the endearments of a wife, or, if he would not accept her as a wife, by the services of a handmaiden. One day, seeing a temple on the top of a mountain, she went towards it, hoping to find there some traces of her lord. Within the temple there were ears of wheat in heaps or twisted into chaplets,[8] there were ears of barley also; there were sickles and all the instruments of harvest. And Psyche, saying to herself, "I may not neglect the shrines, nor the holy service of any God or Goddess, but must strive to win by my works the favor of them all." And so saying she put the sickles and the instruments of harvest, the chaplets and the heaps of grain, into their proper places.

[8] *chaplets:* wreaths

And Ceres, the Goddess of the harvest, found her bending over the tasks she had set herself. She knew her for Psyche, the wife of Cupid. "Ah, Psyche," said the Goddess, "Venus, in her anger, is tracking thy footsteps through the world; she is seeking thee to make thee pay the greatest penalty that can be exacted from thee. And here I find thee taking care of the things that are in my care!" Then Psyche fell at the feet of Ceres, and sweeping the floor with her hair, and washing the feet of the Goddess with her tears, she besought her to have mercy on her. "Suffer me to hide myself for a few days amongst the heaps of grain, till my strength, outworn in my long travail,[9] be recovered by a little rest," she cried. But Ceres answered, "Truly thy tears move me, and I fain would help thee. But I dare not incur the ill-will of my kinswoman. Depart from this as quickly as may be." Then Psyche, filled with a new hopelessness, went away from that temple. Soon, as she went through the half-lighted woods in the valley below, she came to where there was another temple. She saw rich offerings and garments of price hung upon the door-posts and to the branches of the trees, and on them, in letters of gold, were wrought the name of the Goddess to whom they were dedicated. So Psyche went within that temple, and with knees bent and hands laid about the altar, she prayed, "O Juno, sister and spouse of Jupiter, thou art called the Auspicious![10] Be auspicious to my desperate fortune! Willingly dost thou help those in childbirth! Deliver me, therefore — O deliver me from the peril that is upon me!" And as Psyche prayed thus, Juno, in all the majesty of the spouse of Jupiter, appeared before her. And the Goddess, being present, answered, "Would that I might incline to thy prayer; but against the will of Venus whom I have ever loved as a daughter, I may not grant what thou dost ask of me!" Then Psyche went forth from that temple, and filled with more and more dismay, she said to herself, "Whither now shall I take my way? In what solitude can I hide myself from the all-seeing eye of Venus? It is best that I should go before her, and yield myself up to her as to a mistress, and take from her any punishment that even she can inflict upon me." And saying this, Psyche went towards where Venus had her house. And as she

[9] *travail:* painful toil
[10] *Auspicious:* showing hopeful signs

went on she said to herself, "Who knows but I may find him whom my soul seeketh after in the abode of his mother?"

When she came near to the doors of the house of Venus, one of the servants ran out to her, crying, "Hast thou learned at last, wicked maid, that thou hast a mistress?" And seizing Psyche by the hair of her head she dragged her into the presence of the Goddess. And when Venus saw her she laughed, saying, "Thou hast deigned[11] at last to make thy salutations[12] to thy mother-in-law. Now will I see to it that thou makest thyself a dutiful and obedient daughter-in-law."

Saying this she took barley and millet and every kind of grain and seed, and mixed them all together, making a great heap of them. Then she said to Psyche, "Methinks that so plain a maid can only win a lover by the tokens of her industry. Get to work, therefore, and show what thou canst do. Sort this heap of grain, separating the one kind from the other, grain by grain, and see to it that thy task is finished before the evening." Then Venus went from her, and Psyche, appalled by her bidding, was silent and could not put a hand upon the heap. Listlessly[13] she sat beside it and the hours passed. But a little ant came before her; he understood the difficulty of her task and he had pity upon her. He ran hither and thither and summoned the army of the ants. "Have pity," he said to them, "upon the wife of Love, and hasten to help her in her task." Then the host of the insect people gathered together; they sorted the whole heap of grain, separating one kind from the other. And having done this they all departed suddenly.

At nightfall Venus returned; she saw that Psyche's task was finished and she cried out in anger. "The work is not thine; he in whose eyes thou hast found favor surely instructed thee as to how to have it done." She went from Psyche then. But early in the morning she called to her and said, "In the grove yonder, across the torrent, there are sheep whose fleeces shine with gold. Fetch me straightway shreds of that precious stuff, having gotten it in whatever way thou mayst."

---

[11] *deigned:* stooped
[12] *salutations:* respectful greetings
[13] *listlessly:* unable to act

Then Psyche went forth. She stood beside the torrent thinking that she would seek for rest in the depth of it. But from the riverbed the green reed, lowly mother of music, whispered to her and said, "O Psyche! Do not pollute these waters by self-destruction! I will tell thee of a way to get the gold shreds of the fleece of yonder fierce flock. Lie down under yonder plane tree and rest yourself until the coming of evening and the quiet of the river's sound has soothed the flock. Then go amongst the trees that they have been under and gather the shreds of the fleeces from the trees — the leaves hold the golden shreds."

Psyche, instructed by the simple reed, did all that she was told to do. In the quiet of the evening she went into the grove, and she put into her bosom the soft golden stuff that was held by the leaves. Then she returned to where Venus was. The Goddess smiled bitterly upon her, and she said, "Well do I know whence came the instruction that thou hast profited by; but I am not finished with thee yet. Seest thou the utmost peak of yonder mountain? The dark stream which flows down from it waters the Stygian fields, and swells the flood of Cocytus. Bring me now, in this little cruse,[14] a draught from its innermost source." And saying this, Venus put into Psyche's hands a vessel of wrought crystal.

Psyche went up the mountain, but she sought only for a place in which she could bring her life to an end. She came to where there was a rock steep and slippery. From that rock a river poured forth and fell down into an unseen gulf below. And from the rocks on every side serpents came with long necks and unblinking eyes. The very waters found a voice; they said in stifled voices, "What dost thou here?" "Look around thee!" "Destruction is upon thee!" All sense left her, and she stood like one changed into rock.

But the bird of Jupiter took flight to her. He spread his wings over her and said, "Simple one! Didst thou think that thou couldst steal one drop of that relentless stream, the river that is terrible even to the Gods! But give me the vessel." And the eagle took the cruse, and filled it at the source, and returned to her quickly from amongst the raised heads of the serpents.

Then Psyche, receiving the cruse as the gift of life itself, ran back quickly and brought it to Venus. But the angry Goddess was

[14] *cruse:* cup

not yet satisfied. "One task more remains for you to do," she said to Psyche. "Take now this tiny casket, and give it to Proserpine.[15] Tell her that Venus would have of her beauty as much as might suffice for one day's use. Tell her this and take back in the casket what the Queen of Hades will give thee. And be not slow in returning."

Then Psyche perceived that she was now being thrust upon death, and that she would have to go, of her own motion, down to Hades and the Shades. Straightway she climbed to the top of a high tower, thinking to herself, "I will cast myself down hence, and so descend more quickly to the Kingdom of the Dead." But the tower spoke to her and said, "Wretched maiden! If the breath quit thy body, then wilt thou indeed go down to Hades, but by no means return to the upper air again. Listen to me. Not far from this place there is a mountain, and in that mountain there is a hole that is a vent for Hades. Through it is a rough way; following it one comes in a straight course to the castle of Orcus. But thou must not go empty-handed. Take in each hand a morsel of barley bread, soaked in hydromel, and in thy mouth have two pieces of money. When thou art well forward on the way thou wilt overtake a lame ass laden with wood, and a lame driver; he will beg thee to hand to him certain cords to fasten the burden which is falling from the ass: heed him not; pass by him in silence. Thou wilt come to the River of the Dead. Charon, in that leaky bark[16] he hath, will put thee over upon the farther side. Thou shalt deliver to him, for his ferry charge, one of these two pieces of money. But thou must deliver it in such a way that his hand shall take it from between thy lips. As thou art crossing the stream an old man, rising on the water, will put up his moldering hands, and pray thee to draw him into the ferry boat. But beware that thou yield not to unlawful pity.

"When thou art across the stream and upon the level ground, certain gray-haired women, spinning, will cry to thee to lend thy hand to their work. But again beware! Take no part in that spinning! If thou dost thou wilt cast away one of the cakes thou bearest in thine hands. But remember that the loss of either of these cakes will be to thee the loss of the light of day. For a

[15] *Proserpine:* daughter of Ceres whom the god of Hades, Pluto, stole to be his wife.
[16] *bark:* boat

watchdog lies before the threshold of the lonely house of Proserpine. Close his mouth with one of thy cakes, so he will let thee pass. Then thou shalt enter into the presence of Proserpine herself. Do thou deliver thy message, and taking what the Queen of the Dead shall give thee, return back again, offering to the watchdog the other cake, and to the ferryman the other piece of money that thou hast in thy mouth. After this manner mayst thou return again to the light of day. And I charge thee not to look into, nor open, the casket thou bearest with the treasure of the beauty of the divine features hidden therein."

So the stones of the tower spoke. Psyche gave heed to all that they said. She entered the lonely house of Prosperpine. At the feet of the Goddess of the Dead she sat down humbly; she would not rest upon the couch that was there nor take any of the food that was offered her. She delivered her message and she waited. Then Prosperpine filled the casket secretly and shut the lid, and handed it to Psyche. She went from the house; she remembered the sop she had to give the watchdog and the fee she had to give the ferryman. She came back into the light of day. Now even as she hasted into the presence of Venus she said to herself, "I have

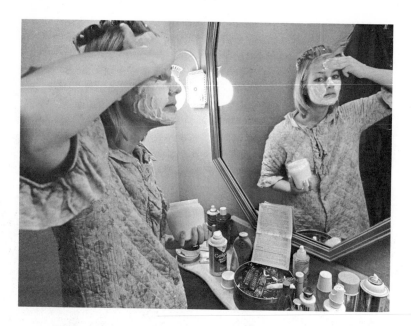

in my hands the divine loveliness. Should I touch myself with a particle of it I should have a beauty indeed that would please him whom I still seek, him whom I still hope to be beside." Saying this, she raised the lid of the casket. Behold! what was within was sleep only, the sleep that was like the sleep of the dead! That sleep overcame Psyche, and she lay upon the ground and moved not.

But now Cupid, being healed of the wound from the burning oil, and longing for Psyche, his beloved, flew from the chamber in his mother's house. He found Psyche lying in slumber. He shook that slumber from her, and awakened her with the point of his arrow. Then he rose upon the air, and he went vehemently[17] upon his way until he came into the highest court of Heaven. There sat Jupiter, the Father of Gods and men. When Cupid went to him, Jupiter took his hand in his, and kissed his face and said to him, "At no time, my son, hast thou regarded me with due honor. With those busy arrows of thine thou hast often upset the harmony that it is mine to bring about. But because thou hast grown up between these hands of mine, I will accomplish thy desire." He bade Mercury[18] call the Gods together. And the Gods

[17] vehemently: with strong feeling
[18] *Mercury:* messenger of the gods

being assembled, Jupiter said to them, "Ye Gods, it seems good to me that this boy should be confined in the bonds of marriage. And he has chosen and embraced a mortal maiden. Let him have the fruit of his love, and possess her forever."

Thereupon the Father of the Gods bade Mercury produce Psyche amongst them. She was brought into the highest court of Heaven. The Father of the Gods held out to her his ambrosial[19] cup. "Drink of it," he said, "and live for ever. Cupid shall never depart from thee." Then the Gods sat down to the marriage feast. On the first couch was the bridegroom with his Psyche at his bosom. Bacchus[20] served wine to the rest of the company, but his own serving boy served it to Jupiter. The Seasons crimsoned all things with their roses. Apollo sang to his lyre. Pan prattled on his reeds. Venus danced very sweetly to the soft music. And thus, with all due rites, did Psyche, born a mortal, become the immortal wife of Love. From Cupid and Psyche was born a daughter whom men call Voluptas.

---

[19] *ambrosial:* Ambrosia was the heavenly drink of the gods.
[20] *Bacchus:* god of wine and feasting

Roll Over

as told by Maria Leach

AMERICAN INDIAN

This is the tale of the old men, the tale of world-making, of making the people. This is the tale I was told.
He lived in the north, did Old Man Madumda, and he thought, "I will make the world."

"How shall I make it?" he thought. "I'll ask my elder brother."

He pulled out four hairs from his head and held them up. "Take me to my brother," he said. He held the hairs to the east, nothing happened. He held the hairs to the north. No. He held them to the west; nothing happened. He held the hairs to the south. The hairs floated. They floated in a circle around Madumda and then started swiftly south. They flashed fire as they flew and Madumda followed, riding in his cloud-house. He smoked his pipe or slept as he traveled, and finally he got there. He arrived at the house of Kuksu, his elder brother.

Four times the hairs swished around the house of Kuksu, then floated in through a little hole, and Madumda followed and entered the house of his brother.

Madumda sat down and smoked his pipe. Four times he put the pipe in his mouth and then passed it to Kuksu. Kuksu took the pipe and smoked it.

"Good will come of this," he said. "It will happen."

Then Madumda scratched off some skin from under his armpit and rolled it into a little ball, which he handed to Kuksu. Kuksu placed it between his big toe and the next. Then Kuksu scraped himself under the armpit and rolled the dead skin into a little ball, which he placed between Madumda's big toe and the next. Madumda then took the ball in his hand and blew upon it four times, and Kuksu also blew four times upon the little ball of skin which Madumda had given him.

Then the brothers took the two little balls and molded them together into one. Kuksu took some of his own hair to mix into it and Madumda did the same.

Then they stood up and turned, facing the six sacred directions: first south, then east, then north, then west, then into the zenith, then down to the nadir.[1]

"Thus everything will be," they said. "There will be people on this earth; there will be food; there will be villages. The people will be many and full of good intentions.

"We shall make the sun, to ripen the food," they said. "We shall give them fire to cook it."

"This is a good plan," said Kuksu. "All will be good."

Then Madumda put the little ball of dried skin into a sack and said he must go.

"Sing your song," he said to Kuksu. And Kuksu sang the long, holy song in the ancient language which nobody understands today. Then Madumda floated homeward to the north, singing his own wishing-song in that old language.

Singing, he tied a string to the little ball which he and Kuksu had made, and strung it through his ear-hole, so that he would not lose it when he went to sleep. For now Madumda slept.

Eight days he slept. He would sleep, wake up, look, see nothing, and go back to sleep. On the eighth day the string jerked and Madumda woke. The little ball had grown big and become the earth.

AND MADUMDA HURLED IT OUT INTO SPACE.

It was dark, so Madumda made the sun. He lighted his pipe and when it was afire he blew the glowing spark into the southern sky. And the spark grew big and became the sun and shed its lovely light over the face of the earth.

Then Madumda walked around in the world, fixing things. "Here a mountain, here some rocks," he said. "Now a valley, a lake, clover growing, acorns on the mountains, juniper and cherries. There must be potatoes and rabbits," he said, "and on that mountain over there, let there be bear, puma, wolf, coyote, fox, skunk; on this one rattlesnakes, kingsnakes, garter snakes."

[1] The zenith is the point in the sky directly overhead and the nadir its opposite, the point directly below an observer in the sphere of the sky.

43

Then Madumda climbed a mountain and on the other side of the mountain it was dark. "Well!" he said. He sat down to think. There was no light here at all. He looked up, and there was light in the sky.

"Roll over," he said to the earth. Madumda turned it over, then turned it back. He rolled the earth over, first one side to the sun, then the other.

"This is the way," he said. "Now it is dark, now it is light; now dark, now light. This is the way." And so it is.

Madumda continued his work. He made rivers, to be roads for the fish; he made a mountain of flint to be arrowheads for the people; he made springs. He planted rushes and bushes, dogwood and willows. "These shall be for the women to weave baskets," he said.

Madumda walked around and came to a lake, and sat down on a log. The lake was calm and smooth. "Don't be like that," said Madumda, "be like this," and he walked into the water and splashed it toward the land. The wind blew and made ripples in the water and the waves ran up on the land and splashed on the rocks.

"That's nice," said Madumda. "That's the way."

Then Madumda thought it was time to make the people. He picked up a few rocks and made some people. They were little short-legged people and stayed in the mountains. Then he made some people out of hair. These had beautiful long black hair. Madumda ate some potatoes to show them how. "This is your food," he said.

Madumda went on and made more people in another place. He made them out of feathers and scattered them all over. These people were covered with feathers. They were bird-people.

Then Madumda pulled four hairs out from under his arm and made some more people. These were covered with hair and had horns on their heads and split hooves. They were deer-people.

Madumda went on and sat on a hill. He took some more hair and scattered it over the hills to make another kind of people. These were big, hairy people with claws, walking about on four legs. They were bear-people. "Are there others besides ourselves?" they asked their maker. "Oh, yes, there will be lots of people," said Madumda. Then he showed them how to eat and went on his way.

Madumda walked northward into the hills and sat down. He reached into his sack and took out some sinew. This he broke into little pieces and scattered the pieces in the hollow between the hills.

"These shall be naked people," he said.

And they were. They were like us. They had hair on their heads but no horns, no feathers or hair on their bodies. They were beautiful and naked and slick in the sunshine.

"Come here," said Madumda, and the people came and listened. "This is your land," said Madumda. "This is where you will live. There is plenty of food. Eat it." He spoke thus and went away.

All these were the first people that Madumda made.

The Story of Ra

as told by Roger Green

EGYPT

In the beginning, before there was any land of Egypt, all was darkness, and there was nothing but a great waste of water called Nu. The power of Nu was such that there arose out of the darkness a great shining egg, and this was Ra.

Now Ra was all-powerful, and he could take many forms. His power and the secret of it lay in his hidden name; but if he spoke other names, that which he named came into being.

"I am Khepera at the dawn, and Ra at noon, and Tum in the evening," he said. And the sun rose and passed across the sky and set for the first time.

Then he named Shu, and the first winds blew; he named Refnut the spitter, and the first rain fell. Next he named Geb, and the earth came into being; he named the goddess Nut, and she was the sky arched over the earth with her feet on one horizon and her hands on the other; he named Hapi, and the great River Nile flowed through Egypt and made it fruitful.

After this Ra named all things that are upon the earth, and they grew. Last of all he named mankind, and there were men and women in the land of Egypt.

Then Ra took on the shape of a man and became the first Pharaoh, ruling over the whole country for thousands and thousands of years, and giving such harvests that for ever afterwards the Egyptians spoke of the good things "which happened in the time of Ra."

But, being in the form of a man, Ra grew old. In time men no longer feared him or obeyed his laws. They laughed at him, saying: "Look at Ra! His bones are like silver, his flesh like gold, his hair is the color of lapis lazuli!" [1]

Ra was angry when he heard this, and he was more angry

[1] *lapis lazuli:* a precious stone

(47)

still at the evil deeds which men were doing in disobedience to his laws. So he called together the gods whom he had made — Shu and Refnut and Geb and Nut — and he also summoned Nu. Soon the gods gathered about Ra in his Secret Place, and the goddesses also. But mankind knew nothing of what was happening, and continued to jeer at Ra and to break his commandments. Then Ra spoke to Nu before the assembled gods: "Eldest of the gods, you who made me; and you gods whom I have made: look upon mankind who came into being at a glance of my Eye. See how men plot against me; hear what they say of me; tell me what I should do to them. For I will not destroy mankind until I have heard what you advise."

Then Nu said: "My son Ra, the god greater than he who made him and mightier than those whom he has created, turn your mighty Eye upon them and send destruction upon them in the form of your daughter the goddess Sekhmet."

Ra answered: "Even now fear is falling upon them and they are fleeing into the deserts and hiding themselves in the mountains in terror at the sound of my voice."

"Send against them the glance of your Eye in the form of Sekhmet!" cried all the other gods and goddesses, bowing before Ra until their foreheads touched the ground.

So at the terrible glance from the Eye of Ra his daughter Sekhmet came into being, the fiercest of all goddesses. Like a lion she rushed upon her prey, and her chief delight was in slaughter and her pleasure was in blood. At the bidding of Ra she came into Upper and Lower Egypt to slay those who had scorned and disobeyed him: she killed them among the mountains which lie on either side of the Nile, and down beside the river, and in the burning deserts. All whom she saw she slew, rejoicing in slaughter and the taste of blood.

Presently Ra looked out over the land and saw what Sekhmet had done. Then he called to her, saying: "Come, my daughter, and tell me how you have obeyed my commands."

Sekhmet answered with the terrible voice of a lioness as she tears her prey: "By the life which you have given me, I have indeed done vengeance on mankind, and my heart rejoices."

Now for many nights the Nile ran red with blood, and Sekhmet's feet were red as she went hither and thither through all the land of Egypt slaying and slaying.

Presently Ra looked out over the earth once more, and now his heart was stirred with pity for men, even though they had rebelled against him. But none could stop the cruel goddess Sekhmet, not even Ra himself: she must cease from slaying of her own accord — and Ra saw that this could only come about through cunning.

So he gave his command: "Bring before me swift messengers who will run upon the earth as silently as shadows and with the speed of the storm winds." When these were brought he said to them: "Go as fast as you can up the Nile to where it flows fiercely over the rocks and among the islands of the First Cataract; go to the isle that is called Elephantine and bring from it a great store of the red ochre[2] which is to be found there."

The messengers sped on their way and returned with the blood-red ochre to Heliopolis, the city of Ra where stand the stone obelisks[3] with points of gold that are like fingers pointing to the sun. It was night when they came to the city, but all day the women of Heliopolis had been brewing beer as Ra bade them.

[2] *ochre:* a kind of earth
[3] *obelisks:* tall, straight monuments

Ra came to where the beer stood waiting in seven thousand jars, and the gods came with him to see how by his wisdom he would save mankind.

"Mingle the red ochre of Elephantine with the barley-beer," said Ra, and it was done, so that the beer gleamed red in the moonlight like the blood of men.

"Now take it to the place where Sekhmet proposes to slay men when the sun rises," said Ra. And while it was still night the seven thousands jars of beer were taken and poured out over the fields so that the ground was covered to the depth of nine inches — three times the measure of the palm of a man's hand — with the strong beer, whose other name is "sleep-maker."

When day came Sekhmet the terrible came also, licking her lips at the thought of the men whom she would slay. She found the place flooded and no living creature in sight; but she saw the beer which was the color of blood, and she thought it was blood indeed — the blood of those whom she had slain.

Then she laughed with joy, and her laughter was like the roar of a lioness hungry for the kill. Thinking that it was indeed blood, she stopped and drank. Again and yet again she drank, laughing with delight; and the strength of the beer mounted to her brain, so that she could no longer slay.

At last she came reeling back to where Ra was waiting; and that day she had not killed even a single man.

Then Ra said: "You come in peace, sweet one." And her name was changed to Hathor, and her nature was changed also to the sweetness of love and the strength of desire. And henceforth Hathor laid low men and women only with the great power of love. But for ever after her priestesses drank in her honor of the beer of Heliopolis colored with the red ochre of Elephantine when they celebrated her festival each New Year.

So mankind was saved, and Ra continued to rule, old though he was. But the time was drawing near when he must leave the earth to reign forever in the heavens, letting the younger gods rule in his place. For dwelling in the form of a man, of a Pharaoh of Egypt, Ra was losing his wisdom; yet he continued to reign, and no one could take his power from him, since that power dwelt in his secret name which none knew but himself. If only anyone could discover his Name of Power, Ra would reign no longer on earth; but only by magic arts was this possible.

Geb and Nut had children: these were the younger gods whose day had come to rule, and their names were Osiris and Isis, Nephthys and Set. Of these Isis was the wisest: she was cleverer than a million men, her knowledge was greater than that of a million of the noble dead. She knew all things in heaven and earth, except only for the Secret Name of Ra, and that she now set herself to learn by guile.[4]

Now Ra was growing older every day. As he passed across the land of Egypt his head shook from side to side with age, his jaw trembled, and he dribbled at the mouth as do the very old among men. As his spittle fell upon the ground it made mud, and this Isis took in her hands and kneaded together as if it had been dough. Then she formed it into the shape of a serpent, making the first cobra — the *uraeus,* which ever after was the symbol of royalty worn by Pharaoh and his queen.

Isis placed the first cobra in the dust of the road by which Ra passed each day as he went through his two kingdoms of Upper and Lower Egypt. As Ra passed by the cobra bit him and then vanished into the grass. But the venom of its bite coursed through

[4] *guile:* clever trickery

(51)

his veins, and for a while Ra was speechless, save for one great cry of pain which rang across the earth from the eastern to the western horizon. The gods who followed him crowded round, asking: "What is it? What ails you?" But he could find no words; his lips trembled and he shuddered in all his limbs, while the poison spread over his body as the Nile spreads over Egypt at the inundation.[5] When at last he could speak, Ra said: "Help me, you whom I have made. Something has hurt me, and I do not know what it is. I created all things, yet this thing I did not make. It is a pain such as I have never known before, and no other pain is equal to it. Yet who can hurt me? — for none knows my Secret Name which is hidden in my heart, giving me all power and guarding me against the magic of both wizard and witch. Nevertheless as I passed through the world which I have created, through the two lands that are my special care, something stung me. It is like fire, yet it is not fire; it is like water and not water. I burn and I shiver, while all my limbs tremble. So call before me all the gods who have skill in healing and knowledge of magic, and wisdom that reaches to the heavens."

Then all the gods came to Ra, weeping and lamenting at the terrible thing which had befallen him. With them came Isis the healer, the queen of magic, who breathes the breath of life and knows words to revive those who are dying. And she said:

"What is it, divine father? Has a snake bitten you? Has a creature of your own creating lifted up its head against you? I will drive it out by the magic that is mine, and make it tremble and fall down before your glory."

"I went by the usual way through my two lands of Egypt," answered Ra, "for I wished to look upon all that I had made. And as I went I was bitten by a snake which I did not see — a snake that I had not created. Now I burn as if with fire and shiver as if my veins were filled with water, and the sweat runs down my face as it runs down the faces of men on the hottest days of summer."

"Tell me your Secret Name," said Isis in a sweet, soothing voice. "Tell it me, divine father; for only by speaking your name in my spells can I cure you."

Then Ra spoke the many names that were his: "I am Maker

[5] *inundation:* flood, yearly in Egypt

of Heaven and Earth," he said. "I am Builder of the Mountains. I am Source of the Waters throughout all the world. I am Light and Darkness. I am Creator of the Great River of Egypt. I am the Kindler of the Fire that burns in the sky; yes, I am Khepera in the morning, Ra at the noontide, and Tum in the evening."

But Isis said never a word, and the poison had its way in the veins of Ra. For she knew that he had told her only the names which all men knew, and that his Secret Name, the Name of Power, still lay hidden in his heart.

At last she said:

"You know well that the name which I need to learn is not among those which you have spoken. Come, tell me the Secret Name, for if you do the poison will come forth and you will have an end of pain."

The poison burned with a great burning, more powerful than any flame of fire, and Ra cried out at last:

"Let the Name of Power pass from my heart into the heart of Isis! But before it does, swear to me that you will tell it to no other save only the son whom you will have, whose name shall be Horus. And bind him first with such an oath that the name will remain with him and be passed on to no other gods or men."

Isis the great magician swore the oath, and the knowledge of the Name of Power passed from the heart of Ra into hers.

Then she said: "By the name which I know, let the poison go from Ra forever!"

So it passed from him and he had peace. But he reigned upon earth no longer. Instead he took his place in the high heavens, traveling each day across the sky in the likeness of the sun itself, and by night crossing the underworld of Amenti in the Boat of Ra and passing through the twelve divisions of Duat where many dangers lurk. Yet Ra passes safely, and with him he takes those souls of the dead who know all the charms and prayers and words that must be said.

Hercules

as told by Edith Hamilton

GREECE

Hercules was the strongest man on earth and he had the supreme self-confidence magnificent physical strength gives. He considered himself on an equality with the gods — and with some reason. They needed his help to conquer the Giants. In the final victory of the Olympians over the brutish sons of Earth, Hercules' arrows played an important part. He treated the gods accordingly. Once when the priestess at Delphi gave no response to the question he asked, he seized the tripod she sat on and declared that he would carry it off and have an oracle[1] of his own. Apollo,[2] of course, would not put up with this, but Hercules was perfectly willing to fight him and Zeus[3] had to intervene. The quarrel was easily settled, however. Hercules was quite good-natured about it. He did not want to quarrel with Apollo, he only wanted an answer from his oracle. If Apollo would give it the matter was settled as far as he was concerned. Apollo on his side, facing this undaunted person, felt an admiration for his boldness and made his priestess deliver the response.

Throughout his life Hercules had this perfect confidence that no matter who was against him he could never be defeated, and facts bore him out. Whenever he fought with anyone the issue was certain beforehand. He could be overcome only by a supernatural force. Hera used hers against him with terrible effect and in the end he was killed by magic, but nothing that lived in the air, sea, or on land ever defeated him.

[1] *oracle:* She was an oracle, that is, she could foretell the future.
[2] *Apollo:* God of music and poetry but also of prophecy and hence of the Delphic oracle.
[3] *Zeus:* Zeus and Hera were the ruling couple of the gods.

54

Intelligence did not figure largely in anything he did and was often conspicuously absent. Once when he was too hot he pointed an arrow at the sun and threatened to shoot him. Another time when the boat he was in was tossed about by the waves he told the waters that he would punish them if they did not grow calm. His intellect was not strong. His emotions were. They were quickly aroused and apt to get out of control, as when he deserted the *Argo* and forgot all about his comrades and the Quest of the Golden Fleece in his despairing grief at losing his young armor-bearer, Hylas. This power of deep feeling in a man of his tremendous strength was oddly endearing, but it worked immense harm, too. He had sudden outbursts of furious anger which were always fatal to the often innocent objects. When the rage had passed and he had come to himself he would show a most disarming penitence and agree humbly to any punishment it was proposed to inflict on him. Without his consent he could not have been punished by anyone — yet nobody ever endured so many punishments. He spent a large part of his life expiating[4] one unfortunate deed after another and never rebelling against the almost impossible demands made upon him. Sometimes he punished himself when others were inclined to exonerate[5] him.

It would have been ludicrous to put him in command of a kingdom as Theseus was put; he had more than enough to do to command himself. He could never have thought out any new or great idea as the Athenian hero was held to have done. His thinking was limited to devising a way to kill a monster which was threatening to kill him. Nevertheless he had true greatness. Not because he had complete courage based upon overwhelming strength, which is merely a matter of course, but because, by his sorrow for wrongdoing and his willingness to do anything to expiate it, he showed greatness of soul. If only he had had some greatness of mind as well, at least enough to lead him along the ways of reason, he would have been the perfect hero.

He was born in Thebes and for a long time was held to be the son of Amphitryon, a distinguished general. In those earlier years he was called Alcides, or descendant of Alcaeus who

[4] *expiating:* repenting
[5] *exonerate:* excuse

was Amphitryon's father. But in reality he was the son of Zeus, who had visited Amphitryon's wife Alcmena in the shape of her husband when the general was away fighting. She bore two children, Hercules to Zeus and Iphicles to Amphitryon. The difference in the boys' descent was clearly shown in the way each acted in face of a great danger which came to them before they were a year old. Hera, as always, was furiously jealous and she determined to kill Hercules.

One evening Alcmena gave both the children their baths and their fill of milk and laid them in their crib, caressing them and saying, "Sleep, my little ones, soul of my soul. Happy be your slumber and happy your awakening." She rocked the cradle and in a moment the babies were asleep. But at darkest midnight when all was silent in the house two great snakes came crawling into the nursery. There was a light in the room and as the two reared up above the crib, with weaving heads and flickering tongues, the children woke, Iphicles screamed and tried to get out of bed, but Hercules sat up and grasped the deadly creatures by the throat. They turned and twisted and wound their coils around his body, but he held them fast. The mother heard Iphicles' screams and, calling to her husband, rushed to the nursery. There sat Hercules laughing, in each hand a long limp body. He gave them gleefully to Amphitryon. They were dead. All knew then that the child was destined to great things. Teiresias, the blind prophet of Thebes, told Alcmena: "I swear that many a Greek woman as she cards the wool at eventide shall sing of this your son and you who bore him. He shall be the hero of all mankind."

Great care was taken with his education, but teaching him what he did not wish to learn was a dangerous business. He seems not to have liked music, which was a most important part of a Greek boy's training, or else he disliked his music master. He flew into a rage with him and brained him with his lute. This was the first time he dealt a fatal blow without intending it. He did not mean to kill the poor musician; he just struck out on the impulse of the moment without thinking, hardly aware of his strength. He was sorry, very sorry, but that did not keep him from doing the same thing again and again. The other subjects he was taught, fencing, wrestling and driving, he took to more kindly, and his teachers in these branches all survived. By the time he was eighteen he was full-grown and he killed, alone by himself, a great lion which lived in the woods of Cithaeron, the Thespian lion. Ever after he wore its skin as a cloak with the head forming a kind of hood over his own head.

His next exploit was to fight and conquer the Minyans, who had been exacting[6] a burdensome tribute from the Thebans. The grateful citizens gave him as a reward the hand of the Princess Megara. He was devoted to her and to their children and yet this marriage brought upon him the greatest sorrow of his life as well as trials and dangers such as no one ever went through, before or after. When Megara had borne him three sons he went mad. Hera who never forgot a wrong sent the madness upon him. He killed his children and Megara, too, as she tried to protect the youngest. Then his sanity returned. He found himself in his bloodstained hall, the dead bodies of his sons and his wife beside him. He had no idea what had happened, how they had been killed. Only

[6] *exacting:* requiring

a moment since, as it seemed to him, they had all been talking together. As he stood there in utter bewilderment the terrified people who were watching him from a distance saw that the mad fit was over, and Amphitryon dared to approach him. There was no keeping the truth from Hercules. He had to know how this horror had come to pass and Amphitryon told him. Hercules heard him out; then he said, "And I myself am the murderer of my dearest."

"Yes," Amphitryon answered trembling. "But you were out of your mind."

Hercules paid no attention to the implied excuse.

"Shall I spare my own life then?" he said. "I will avenge upon myself these deaths."

But before he could rush out and kill himself, even as he started to do so, his desperate purpose was changed and his life was spared. This miracle — it was nothing less — of recalling Hercules, from frenzied feeling and violent action to sober reason and sorrowful acceptance, was not wrought by a god descending from the sky. It was a miracle caused by human friendship. His friend Theseus stood before him and stretched out his hands to clasp those bloodstained hands. Thus according to the common Greek idea he would himself become defiled[7] and have a part in Hercules' guilt.

"Do not start back," he told Hercules. "Do not keep me from sharing all with you. Evil I share with you is not evil to me. And hear me. Men great of soul can bear the blows of heaven and not flinch."

Hercules said, "Do you know what I have done?"

"I know this," Theseus answered. "Your sorrows reach from earth to heaven."

"So I will die," said Hercules.

"No hero spoke those words," Theseus said.

"What can I do but die?" Hercules cried. "Live? A branded man, for all to say, 'Look. There is he who killed his wife and sons!' Everywhere my jailers, the sharp scorpions of the tongue!"

"Even so, suffer and be strong," Theseus answered. "You shall come to Athens with me, share my home and all things with me. And you will give to me and to the city a great return, the glory of having helped you."

[7] *defiled:* morally soiled

A long silence followed. At last Hercules spoke, slow, heavy words. "So let it be," he said "I will be strong and wait for death."

The two went to Athens, but Hercules did not stay there long. Theseus, the thinker, rejected the idea that a man could be guilty of murder when he had not known what he was doing and that those who helped such a one could be reckoned defiled. The Athenians agreed and welcomed the poor hero. But he himself could not understand such ideas. He could not think the thing out at all; he could only feel. He had killed his family. Therefore he was defiled and a defiler of others. He deserved that all should turn from him with loathing. At Delphi where he went to consult the oracle, the priestess looked at the matter just as he did. He needed to be purified, she told him, and only a terrible penance could do that. She bade him go to his cousin Eurystheus, King of Mycenae (of Tiryns in some stories) and submit to whatever he demanded of him. He went willingly, ready to do anything that could make him clean again. It is plain from the rest of the story that the priestess knew what Eurystheus was like and that he would beyond question purge[8] Hercules thoroughly.

Eurystheus was by no means stupid, but of a very ingenious turn of mind, and when the strongest man on earth came to him humbly prepared to be his slave, he devised a series of penances[9] which from the point of view of difficulty and danger could not have been improved upon. It must be said, however, that he was helped and urged on by Hera. To the end of Hercules' life she never forgave him for being Zeus's son. The tasks Eurystheus gave him to do are called "the Labors of Hercules." There were twelve of them and each one was all but impossible.

The first was to kill the lion of Nemea, a beast no weapons could wound. That difficulty Hercules solved by choking the life out of him. Then he heaved the huge carcass up on his back and carried it into Mycenae. After that, Eurystheus, a cautious man, would not let him inside the city. He gave him his orders from afar.

The second labor was to go to Lerna and kill a creature with nine heads called the Hydra which lived in a swamp there.

[8] *purge:* cleanse
[9] *penances:* ways of working off guilt

60

This was exceedingly hard to do, because one of the heads was immortal and the others almost as bad, inasmuch as when Hercules chopped off one, two grew up instead. However, he was helped by his nephew Iolaus who brought him a burning brand with which he seared the neck as he cut each head off so that it could not sprout again. When all had been chopped off he disposed of the one that was immortal by burying it securely under a great rock.

The third labor was to bring back alive a stag with horns of gold, sacred to Artemis, which lived in the forests of Cerynitia. He could have killed it easily, but to take it alive was another matter and he hunted it a whole year before he succeeded.

The fourth labor was to capture a great boar which had its lair on Mount Erymanthus. He chased the beast from one place to another until it was exhausted; then he drove it into deep snow and trapped it.

The fifth labor was to clean the Augean stables in a single day. Augeas had thousands of cattle and their stalls had not been cleared out for years. Hercules diverted the courses of two rivers and made them flow through the stables in a great flood that washed out the filth in no time at all.

The sixth labor was to drive away the Stymphalian birds, which were a plague to the people of Stymphalus because of their enormous numbers. He was helped by Athena to drive them out of their coverts, and as they flew up he shot them.

The seventh labor was to go to Crete and fetch from there the beautiful savage bull that Poseidon[10] had given Minos.[11] Hercules mastered him, put him in a boat and brought him to Eurystheus.

The eighth labor was to get the man-eating mares of King Diomedes of Thrace. Hercules slew Diomedes first and then drove off the mares unopposed.

The ninth labor was to bring back the girdle of Hippolyta, the Queen of the Amazons. When Hercules arrived she met him kindly and told him she would give him the girdle, but Hera stirred up trouble. She made the Amazons think that Hercules was going to carry off their queen, and they charged down on his ship. Hercules, without a thought of how kind Hippolyta had been, without any thought at all, instantly killed her, taking it for granted that she was responsible for the attack. He was able to fight off the others and get away with the girdle.

The tenth labor was to bring back the cattle of Geryon, who was a monster with three bodies living on Erythia, a western island. On his way there Hercules reached the land at the end of the Mediterranean and he set up as a memorial of his journey two great rocks, called the Pillars of Hercules (now Gibraltar and Ceuta). Then he got the oxen and took them to Mycenae.

The eleventh labor was the most difficult of all so far. It was to bring back the Golden Apples of the Hesperides, and he did not know where they were to be found. Atlas, who bore the vault of heaven upon his shoulders, was the father of the Hesperides, so Hercules went to him and asked him to get the apples for him. He offered to take upon himself the burden of the sky while Atlas was away. Atlas, seeing a chance of being relieved forever from his heavy task, gladly agreed. He came

[10] *Poseidon:* God of the sea
[11] *Minos:* King of Crete

back with the apples, but he did not give them to Hercules. He told Hercules he could keep on holding up the sky, for Atlas himself would take the apples to Eurystheus. On this occasion Hercules had only his wits to trust to; he had to give all his strength to supporting that mighty load. He was successful, but because of Atlas' stupidity rather than his own cleverness. He agreed to Atlas' plan, but asked him to take the sky back for just a moment so that Hercules could put a pad on his shoulders to ease the pressure. Atlas did so, and Hercules picked up the apples and went off.

The twelfth labor was the worst of all. It took him down to the lower world, and it was then that he freed Theseus from the Chair of Forgetfulness. His task was to bring Cerberus, the three-headed dog, up from Hades. Pluto gave him permission provided Hercules used no weapons to overcome him. He could use his hands only. Even so, he forced the terrible monster to submit to him. He lifted him and carried him all the way up to the earth and on to Mycenae. Eurystheus very sensibly did not want to keep him and made Hercules carry him back. This was his last labor.

When all were completed and full expiation made for the death of his wife and children, he would seem to have earned ease and tranquillity for the rest of his life. But it was not so. He was never tranquil and at ease. An exploit quite as difficult as most of the labors was the conquest of Antaeus, a Giant and a mighty wrestler who forced strangers to wrestle with him on condition that if he was victor he should kill them. He was roofing a temple with the skulls of his victims. As long as he could touch the earth he was invincible. If thrown to the ground he sprang up with renewed strength from the contact. Hercules lifted him up and holding him in the air strangled him.

Story after story is told of his adventures. He fought the river-god Achelous because Achelous was in love with the girl Hercules now wanted to marry. Like everyone else by this time, Achelous had no desire to fight him and he tried to reason with him. But that never worked with Hercules. It only made him more angry. He said, "My hand is better than my tongue. Let me win fighting and you may win talking." Achelous took the form of a bull and attacked him fiercely, but

63

Hercules was used to subduing bulls. He conquered him and broke off one of his horns. The cause of the contest, a young princess named Deianira, became his wife.

He traveled to many lands and did many other great deeds. At Troy he rescued a maiden who was in the same plight as Andromeda, waiting on the shore to be devoured by a sea monster which could be appeased in no other way. She was the daughter of King Laomedon, who had cheated Apollo and Poseidon of their wages after at Zeus's command they had built for the King the walls of Troy. In return Apollo sent a pestilence,[12] and Poseidon the sea serpent. Hercules agreed to rescue the girl if her father would give him the horses Zeus had given his grandfather. Laomedon promised, but when Hercules had slain the monster the King refused to pay. Hercules captured the city, killed the King, and gave the maiden to his friend, Telamon of Salamis, who had helped him.

On his way to Atlas to ask him about the Golden Apples, Hercules came to the Caucasus, where he freed Prometheus, slaying the eagle that preyed on him.

Along with these glorious deeds there were others not glorious. He killed with a careless thrust of his arm a lad who was serving him by pouring water on his hands before a feast. It was an accident and the boy's father forgave Hercules, but Hercules could not forgive himself and he went into exile for a time. Far worse was his deliberately slaying a good friend in order to avenge an insult offered him by the young man's father. King Eurytus. For this base action Zeus himself punished him: he sent him to Lydia to be a slave to the Queen, Omphale, some say for a year, some for three years. She amused herself with him, making him at times dress up as a woman and do woman's work, weave or spin. He submitted patiently, as always, but he felt himself degraded by this servitude and with complete unreason blamed Eurytus for it and swore he would punish him to the utmost when he was freed.

All the stories about him are characteristic, but the one which gives the clearest picture of him is the account of a visit he made when he was on his way to get the man-eating mares of Diomedes, one of the twelve labors. The house he had

[12] *pestilence:* disease, plague

planned to spend a night in, that of his friend Admetus, a king in Thessaly, was a place of deep mourning when he came to it although he did not know. Admetus had just lost his wife in a very strange way.

The cause of her death went back into the past, to the time when Apollo in anger at Zeus for killing his son Aesculapius killed Zeus's workmen, the Cyclopes. He was punished by being forced to serve on earth as a slave for a year and Admetus was the master he chose or Zeus chose for him. During his servitude Apollo made friends with the household, especially with the head of it and his wife Alcestis. When he had an opportunity to prove how strong his friendship was he took it. He learned that the three Fates had spun all of Admetus' thread of life, and were on the point of cutting it. He obtained from them a respite.[13] If someone would die in Admetus' stead, he could live. This news he took to Admetus, who at once set about finding a substitute for himself. He went first quite confidently to his father and mother. They were old and they were devoted to him. Certainly one or the other would consent to take his place in the world of the dead. But to his astonishment he found they would not. They told him, "God's daylight is sweet even to the old. We do not ask you to die for us. We will not die for you." And they were completely unmoved by his angry contempt: "You, standing palsied at the gate of death and yet afraid to die!"

He would not give up, however. He went to his friends begging one after another of them to die and let him live. He evidently thought his life was so valuable that someone would surely save it even at the cost of the supreme sacrifice. But he met with an invariable refusal. At last in despair he went back to his house and there he found a substitute. His wife Alcestis offered to die for him. No one who has read so far will need to be told that he accepted the offer. He felt exceedingly sorry for her and still more for himself in having to lose so good a wife, and he stood weeping beside her as she died. When she was gone he was overwhelmed with grief and decreed that she should have the most magnificent of funerals.

It was at this point that Hercules arrived, to rest and enjoy himself under a friend's roof on his journey north to Diomedes.

[13] *respite:* a holding off of fate, a reprieve

The way Admetus treated him shows more plainly than any other story we have how high the standards of hospitality were, how much was expected from a host to a guest.

As soon as Admetus was told of Hercules' arrival, he came to meet him with no appearance of mourning except in his dress. His manner was that of one gladly welcoming a friend. To Hercules' question who was dead he answered quietly that a woman of his household, but no relative of his, was to be buried that day. Hercules instantly declared that he would not trouble him with his presence at such a time, but Admetus steadily refused to let him go elsewhere. "I will not have you sleep under another's roof," he told him. To his servants he said that the guest was to be taken to a distant room where he could hear no sounds of grief, and given dinner and lodging there. No one must let him know what had happened.

Hercules dined alone, but he understood that Admetus must as a matter of form attend the funeral and the fact did not stand in the way of his enjoying himself. The servants left at home to attend to him were kept busy satisfying his enormous appetite and, still more, refilling his wine-jug. Hercules became very happy and very drunk and very noisy. He roared out songs at the top of his voice, some of them highly objectionable songs, and behaved himself in a way that was nothing less than indecent at the time of a funeral. When the servants looked their disapproval he shouted at them not to be so solemn. Couldn't they give him a smile now and then like good fellows? Their gloomy faces took away his appetite. "Have a drink with me," he cried, "many drinks."

One of them answered timidly that it was not a time for laughter and drinking.

"Why not?" thundered Hercules. "Because a stranger woman is dead?"

"A stranger — " faltered the servant.

"Well, that's what Admetus told me," Hercules said angrily. "I suppose you won't say he lied to me."

"Oh, no," the servant answered. "Only — he's too hospitable. But please have some more wine. Our trouble is only our own."

He turned to fill the winecup but Hercules seized him — and no one ever disregarded that grasp.

"There's something strange here," he said to the frightened man. "What is wrong?"

"You see for yourself we are in mourning," the other answered.

"But why, man why?" Hercules cried. "Has my host made a fool of me? Who is dead?"

"Alcestis," the servant whispered. "Our Queen."

There was a long silence. Then Hercules threw down his cup.

"I might have known," he said. "I saw he had been weeping. His eyes were red. But he swore it was a stranger. He made me come in. Oh, good friend and good host. And I — got drunk, made merry, in this house of sorrow. Oh, he should have told me."

Then he did as always, he heaped blame upon himself. He had been a fool, a drunken fool, when the man he cared for was crushed with grief. As always, too, his thoughts turned quickly to find some way of atoning. What could he do to make amends? There was nothing he could not do. He was perfectly sure of that, but what was there which would help his friend? Then light dawned on him. "Of course," he said to himself. "That is the way. I must bring Alcestis back from the dead. Of course. Nothing could be clearer. I'll find that old fellow, Death. He is sure to be near her tomb and I'll wrestle with him. I will crack his body between my arms until he gives her to me. If he is not by the grave I will go down to Hades after him. Oh, I will return good to my friend who has been so good to me." He hurried out exceedingly pleased with himself and enjoying the prospect of what promised to be a very good wrestling match.

When Admetus returned to his empty and desolate house Hercules was there to greet him, and by his side was a woman. "Look at her, Admetus," he said. "Is she like anyone you know?" And when Admetus cried out, "A ghost! Is it a trick — some mockery of the gods?" Hercules answered, "It is your wife. I fought Death for her and I made him give her back."

There is no other story about Hercules which shows so clearly his character as the Greeks saw it: his simplicity and blundering stupidity; his inability not to get roaring drunk in a house where someone was dead; his quick penitence and desire to make amends at no matter what cost; his perfect confidence that not even Death was his match. That is the portrait of Hercules. To be sure, it would have been still more accurate if it had shown him in a fit of rage killing one of the servants who were annoying him with their gloomy faces, but the poet Euripides from whom we get the story kept it clear of everything that did not bear directly on Alcestis' death and return to life. Another death or two, however natural when Hercules was present, would have blurred the picture he wanted to paint.

As Hercules had sworn to do while he was Omphale's slave, no sooner was he free than he started to punish King Eurytus because he himself had been punished by Zeus for killing Eurytus' son. He collected an army, captured the King's city and put him to death. But Eurytus, too, was avenged, for indirectly this victory was the cause of Hercules' own death.

Before he had quite completed the destruction of the city, he sent home — where Deianira, his devoted wife, was waiting for him to come back from Omphale in Lydia — a band of captive maidens, one of them especially beautiful, Iole, the King's daughter. The man who brought them to Deianira told her that Hercules was madly in love with this Princess. This news was not so hard for Deianira as might be expected, because she believed she had a powerful love-charm which she had kept for years against just such an evil, a woman in her own house preferred before her. Directly after her marriage, when Hercules was taking her home, they had reached a river where the Centaur Nessus acted as ferryman, carrying travelers over the water. He took Deianira on his back and in midstream insulted her. She shrieked and Hercules shot the beast as he reached the other bank. Before he died he told Deianira to take some of his blood and use it as a charm for Hercules if ever he loved another woman more than her. When she heard about Iole, it seemed to her the time had come, and she anointed a splendid robe with the blood and sent it to Hercules by the messenger.

As the hero put it on, the effect was the same as that of the robe Medea had sent her rival whom Jason was about to marry. A fearful pain seized him, as though he were in a burning fire. In his first agony he turned on Deianira's messenger, who was, of course, completely innocent, seized him and hurled him down into the sea. He could still slay others, but it seemed that he himself could not die. The anguish he felt hardly weakened him. What had instantly killed the young Princess of Corinth could not kill Hercules. He was in torture, but he lived and they brought him home. Long before, Deianira had heard what her gift had done to him and had killed herself. In the end he did the same. Since death would not come to him, he would go to death. He ordered those around him to build a great pyre on Mount Octa and carry him to it. When at last he reached it he knew that now he could die and he was glad. "This is rest," he said. "This is the end." And as they lifted him to the pyre he lay down on it as one who at a banquet table lies down upon his couch.

He asked his youthful follower, Philoctetes, to hold the torch to set the wood on fire; and he gave him his bow and arrows, which were to be far-famed in the young man's hands, too, at Troy. Then the flames rushed up and Hercules was seen no more on earth. He was taken to heaven, where he was reconciled to Hera and married her daughter Hebe, and where

> *After his mighty labors he has rest.*
> *His choicest prize eternal peace*
> *Within the homes of blessedness.*

But it is not easy to imagine him contentedly enjoying rest and peace, or allowing the blessed gods to do so, either.

Thor's Journey to Utgard

as told by Barbara Picard

SCANDINAVIA

Thor was the Norse or Scandinavian god of thunder, war and strength, son of Odin, and carried a magic hammer. Thursday is named for him. Loki was the god of confusion and mischief.

In company with Loki, and not alone as was more usual for him, Thor once set out for Iotunheim to seek adventure. He took with him Miollnir, his great hammer, and his belt that increased his strength twofold, and he and Loki traveled in his chariot that was drawn by his two goats.

Towards evening they came to the home of a poor farmer who offered them shelter for the night, not knowing who they might be. But he had not in his house enough meat to feed two guests, and ashamed by his poverty, he apologized for the meager fare which was all that he could give to the strangers.

Thor smiled. "There is a remedy for that, good farmer," he said. And unharnessing his goats from the chariot, he slew them both. "There lies meat enough for us all," he said. "Flay[1] them and bid your good wife busy herself with the cooking, and so shall there be an ample meal for two hungry travelers and for you and your family besides."

So helped by his son, Thialfi, the farmer flayed the goats, and his wife prepared the goat flesh for their supper.

[1] *flay:* skin

72

"Lay the hides away from the fire, lest they are burnt," warned Thor. "And then, as we eat, let us cast on to them the bones of the goats, taking care that none are broken."

Soon a fine supper was ready, and they all sat down to eat. There was goats' meat in plenty, well roasted, and new-baked bread; and while the bones were picked clean and tossed aside on the goatskins and the ale cups were refilled time after time from the vat, the meal passed with much mirth and enjoyment. Thor with his huge tawny beard and his great appetite made the rafters ring with his mighty laughter at red-haired Loki's sly jesting, until the farmer and his wife thought that never had they entertained two more pleasing guests.

The youth Thialfi, his head a little heavy from the ale that he had drunk, holding a thighbone of one of the goats, looked at it longingly and wished that he might break it to eat the marrow, and wondered why his father's loud-laughing guest should take so much care to have the bones kept whole. He sighed at the thought of wasting a marrow such as was not come by every day in a house where there was poverty; and then he looked up to see that the handsome, red-haired other stranger was watching him with a little smile, from his seat beside the fire.

"And why not, lad?" asked Loki quietly. "What is there against it? The marrow in that bone would be well worth eating."

Thialfi blushed that his thoughts had been guessed aright, and he looked away. But a few moments later he raised his eyes again and saw that Loki was still watching him, and it seemed to him that Loki's smile was now a little touched with scorn. "Am I a child, that I should be afraid to disobey a foolish order?" thought Thialfi, and with a quick glance to see that no one else was watching him, he took up his knife and split the bone and ate the marrow out of it. And from the hearth he heard Loki laugh, very quietly.

In the morning, Thor rose up before any of the others were awake, and taking Miollnir, he touched the goathides and the bones lightly with the hammer, and immediately the goats stood up, alive and whole. But then Thor saw that one of them was lame in a hind leg. His angry shouts roused the others. "Someone has broken a bone of my goat," he said, and his voice thundered through the little house, as he swung his hammer above his head.

"It is Thor. It is Thor himself, and could be no other,"

cried the farmer to his wife. And trembling and fearful, he and his family knelt before Thor and implored his pardon for whatever wrong they might have done. And no one of them was more afraid than young Thialfi.

But Loki stood calmly by the ashes of the hearth and smiled to himself at the uproar.

"Take all that we have, great one, but spare us," pleaded the farmer. 'It is little enough that I have to offer you, for I am a poor man. Yet will I give you the best that I have in recompense. Take my son Thialfi to be your servant. Though young, he is strong, and no man can run as fast as he. He will serve you faithfully. Only spare us all, I beg of you."

At their terror and their distress, Thor's anger cooled and he laid Miollnir by. "I will take your son," he said, "and may I find him as loyal and as willing as you declare him to be." And at his words there was joy in the little house once more.

Leaving his goats and his chariot in the care of the farmer and his wife, Thor continued on his way to Iotunheim, striding off with great steps, with Loki at his side, and followed by Thialfi bearing food for the journey.

After a time they crossed the sea into Iotunheim, and went on eastwards through the giants' land, and when night fell they had not yet found anywhere to shelter. But going on a little way in the darkness, they saw before them the shape of a large building with an entrance at one end, very wide and high. Going through this entrance, they found themselves in a hall, and receiving no answer to their calls, they lay down in the darkness and were soon asleep.

But at about midnight they were all three awakened by a great shaking of the earth, and the walls of the house trembled as though they might at any moment fall. Thor jumped up and cried out to his companions, and together they groped around in the darkness of the hall until they came upon a smaller room leading from it, and here they remained, Thor sitting in the doorway with Miollnir held across his knees. The earth had by this time ceased to tremble, but soon there came a noise as of thunder close by, and this continued unbroken until the dawn.

When it was light, Thor went out from the house and saw, lying on the ground near by, an enormous man, and it was this giant's snoring that had sounded as though it were a thunder-

storm, and his lying down to rest that had caused the earth to shake. Thor girded on his belt that increased his strength twofold, and gripping Miollnir tightly, he went over to the giant; but as he approached, the huge man awoke and sat up and looked at him.

"Who are you, large stranger?" asked Thor.

"I am called Skrymir," answered the giant, "and I have no need to ask your name, for I do not doubt from your appearance that you are Thor himself. Am I not right?"

"I am indeed Thor of the Aesir."

Skrymir yawned and stretched his arms. "Good morning to you, Thor," he said. And then he caught sight of his glove, lying a little way off. "Why, Thor," he said, "what have you been doing with my glove?" And he put out his hand to pick it up, and Thor saw that it was no less than the giant's glove which, in the darkness, he and the others had taken for a house; and as for the little room where they had hidden from the earthquake, it had been the thumb of the glove.

"Whither are you bound, my friend?" asked Skrymir.

"We go to the fortress which is called Utgard," replied Thor.

Skrymir was silent for a moment, then he asked, "Since you seem to be journeying even in the same direction as I myself, will you not give me your company along the way, Thor, and you too, red-haired Loki?"

"Willingly," said the two gods.

So first they settled down to eat their morning meal, Thor and his companions from the bag which Thialfi had carried, and the giant from his own huge sack. And after they had eaten, Skrymir proposed that the others should give him their food to carry as well as his own, and they dropped their bag into the sack and he tied up the sack and slung it over his back, and they all set off together.

At evening they reached a grove of great oak trees, and here Skrymir suggested that they might shelter for the night, and on the others' assenting, he flung down his sack of food, saying, "I am tired and I would sleep. Let you share out the food, Thor." And with that he lay down and was soon snoring like a thunderstorm.

Thor took the sack. "Even if you have no wish to eat, good Skrymir," he said, "we others are hungry." And he made to open the sack and take out the food. But try as he might, he could find no way to loosen the knots of the thongs with which it was tied; and after a time he became mightily angered at the waste of labor, and taking up Miollnir, he went to where Skrymir lay, and swinging the hammer, smote him on the head. Skrymir rolled over and opened his eyes and asked sleepily, "What is the matter, Thor? It seems to me as though a leaf has fallen on my head and woken me, or was it you who wakened me to tell me you had eaten and were about to go to rest?"

And Thor was ashamed that his great blow had seemed no more to the giant than the fall of an oak leaf, and he said, "We have indeed eaten and are about to lie down to sleep. Good night to you, Skrymir."

Supperless, Thor and Loki lay down under another tree with Thialfi close by, and none too happy in their minds at the thought of their traveling companion, they fell asleep, for they were tired.

At midnight Thor was awakened by the sound of Skrymir's mighty snoring, and could not go to sleep again by reason of the noise. He bore it for as long as he could, and then arose, and taking Miollnir, went again to where the giant lay, and struck him upon the head an even greater blow than the last that he had dealt him, and Miollnir sank deep into the giant's brow.

But Skrymir only awoke and opened his eyes and said, "Why, are you there, Thor? An acorn must have dropped from the oak tree and woken me. It is dark, surely it is not yet time to rise?"

And Thor, ashamed that such a mighty stroke had seemed no more to Skrymir than an acorn fallen from a bough, said, "It is no later than midnight, Skrymir. There is yet time for us to sleep."

But Thor slept no more that night. Instead he lay and wondered how he might destroy a giant so powerful that even Miollnir seemed a harmless weapon against him. "For," he thought, "it were best that such a one, who may yet prove an enemy to Asgard, however well disposed he now may be, should not be allowed to escape." And a little before dawn, hearing from his snores that Skrymir was still sound asleep, Thor once more took up Miollnir and went to where the giant lay. And then, with all his strength, he crashed his mighty hammer down upon the giant's upturned temple, and he saw it sink in, even to the haft.

But Skrymir only sat up and passed his hand across his cheek and said, "The birds must be nesting in this tree, for I thought I felt a twig fall upon my head."

And Thor was silent, angry and ashamed that the strongest of the gods had proved so puny in power against one who came from Iotunheim.

Skrymir rose and said, "Our ways must part here, Thor and red-haired Loki, for I must go north towards the hills, and to the east lies the fortress which is called Utgard, where you wish to go. But before we part, let me give to you a word of good advice. I have marked how you three have whispered among yourselves that I am tall and broad and that my strength is great, but in Utgard there are others taller and broader and mightier in strength by far than I. Therefore it were well if, when you come to Utgard and meet its lord, you do not boast of your small prowess."[2] He paused and laughed. "Best would it be, little Thor, if you went not on to Utgard, but turned back here. Yet if go

[2] *prowess:* great skill

there you must, take care that you heed well what I have said.
Farewell." Then, picking up his sack of food, Skrymir slung it
over his shoulder and strode away towards the hills. And Thor
and Loki and the farmer's son were not sorry to see him go.

"What say you," asked Thor, "do we pay heed to his words
and go back, or do we go on, as we had intended?"

Loki, ever ready for an adventure, smiled. "We go on," he
said, "for I am hungry, and that Skrymir has taken all our food
with him."

So they went on together, and at midday they came to a
plain on which stood a huge fortress, so high that they had to
stretch their necks and bend their heads backwards to see the top
of it. When they came up to this fortress, they found that it had a
massive gate of iron bars which was locked fast. But so tall and
wide was the gate, that Thor and his companions were easily able
to slip in between the bars and so come into the courtyard. The
house door being open, they went into the great hall, and it was
indeed a vast room, with a bench running along each side, and
on the benches many giants sitting at meat. And at the end of the
hall, on the high seat, sat the lord of Utgard himself.

78

Thor and Loki went boldly up to him and greeted him. He looked them up and down and smiled in scorn. "It seems, from what I have heard of his appearance, that you must be Thor from Asgard," he said. "But, oh, what a tiny weakling seems this great Thor of whom I have heard so much. Come now, strangers, are you skilled at any feats? For no one who is not greater than his fellows at some one thing or another sits down to eat in Utgard. What say you, have you any craft or skill?"

And while Thor hesitated, remembering how small his strength had seemed beside the might of Skrymir, Loki spoke. "I am hungry," he said, "and I have waited long for this morning's meal. I will warrant that there is no one here who can eat more quickly than I, when once good food is set before me."

The lord of Utgard laughed. "We shall soon try you, red-haired Loki," he said, "to see whether you boast without good reason." And he called down the hall to one of his servants who was named Logi, that he should match himself against his master's guest, to see who could eat more quickly.

A great trough filled high with roasted meat was carried in and set down in the hall; and Loki threw off his cloak and tossed back his flaming hair, and sat at one end of the trough, with the giant Logi at the other; and at a sign from the lord of Utgard, they both began to eat at once. And each of them ate as fast as he was able, so that they both came face to face in the middle of the trough and all the meat was gone. Loki looked up. "What think you of that for an appetite?" he asked.

But the lord of Utgard pointed to the trough and said, "It was not ill done, but see, my servant can do better." And Loki saw that the giant had eaten not only all the meat off the bones, but the bones and his half of the trough as well.

And all the giants in the great hall laughed, and none so loudly as their lord. And Thor frowned in anger and reddened in shame that the gods had been worsted yet again by those from Iotunheim. But Loki only shrugged his shoulders and said, "Nevertheless, it was a good meal, and I enjoyed it greatly."

Then the lord of Utgard turned again to Thor and said, "Come, Thor, what of your other companion? In what does he excel?" He pointed to Thialfi. "That youth there, is there anything at which he is more accomplished than any other man?"

"I have never yet been beaten by any other man when the

fleetness of my foot was in the question," said Thialfi. "Match me against any of your runners, and I will undertake to win a race on any course you choose."

The lord of Utgard smiled. "You must indeed run swiftly if that is so," he said. "But let us go out to the courtyard and see you prove your words."

They all went forth from the house to the huge courtyard, which was as wide as any field, and there the lord of Utgard called out a youth named Hugi and bade him run against Thialfi. "Let them run three times," he said.

So they ran together once across the courtyard from end to end. And when Hugi reached the farther wall, he was so far ahead of Thialfi that he turned back and ran a little way to meet him.

"That was well run, Thialfi," said the lord of Utgard. "I think that never has there come here a man who could run so fast as you. Yet do you not run fast enough to beat my Hugi."

They ran a second time, and when Hugi reached the farther wall, Thialfi was little more than halfway along the course.

"You run well, Thialfi," said the lord of Utgard, "but I do not think that you will win this race."

And Thialfi and the giant lad ran a third time; and when Hugi had reached the farther wall, Thialfi was not yet halfway across the courtyard. And a great cheer went up from the men of Utgard, for Hugi the winner.

"The sport has made me thirsty," laughed their lord. "Come, let us go back into the house and drink. And perhaps there is some small thing at which you, great Thor, are skilled, that you may prove youself to us of Utgard?"

"I can drink with anyone," said Thor, "and drink more deeply."

"Well said," laughed the lord of Utgard. And he called to his serving boy to bring his drinking horn. "If this horn is drained in one draught," he said, "it is considered that the drinker drinks well, and well enough if it is drained in two. But no one here is so poor a drinker that he cannot drain the horn in three."

Thor looked at the horn and thought that though long, it was not so very large, and he was thirsty. "I shall drink it all off easily in one draught," he said to himself, and raised the horn to his lips. But though he drank deeply and until his breath failed him, when he came to look into the horn, it seemed as though there were yet a great deal within to be drunk.

"If anyone had told me," said the lord of Utgard, "that great Thor could not empty my horn in one draught, I should have called him a liar. But now have I seen it with my own eyes. Yet have I no doubt that a second draught will empty it."

Thor did not answer him, instead he put the horn to his lips again and drank an even mightier draught than the first. But when he had to pause for breath, and he looked into the horn, it seemed as though he had drunk but very little.

"Come, Thor," said the lord of Utgard, "you may be reckoned a mighty drinker among the Aesir, but not so here. Yet surely you will not fail to empty my horn at a third attempt?"

Then Thor grew very angry and he determined to succeed, and he drank for a third time with all his might. But when he paused and looked into the horn once more, though the drink was certainly less, still was there much left to be finished. And Thor handed back the horn to the serving boy and would not drink again, while the lord of Utgard laughed.

"It seems that you are no mighty drinker when judged by our men," he said. "But tell me what else you can do."

"Such draughts would not be considered mean in Asgard," said Thor, "and there, too, is my strength considered great enough. Try me with some feat of strength, and I will not fail in that."

"There is a little thing which our youths here find much sport in doing," said the lord of Utgard, "and it is such a little thing that I should not dare to suggest that the great Thor should try it, had I not seen for myself that he is less mighty than I had ever supposed him to be."

"What thing is this?" asked Thor, frowning.

"No more than to lift up my cat from the floor," said the lord of Utgard. And as he spoke there came into the hall a large gray cat.

Thor looked at it. "That were easily done," he said. "It is but a cat, though it is large." And he went to it and put his hands below it and made to pick it up. But the cat arched itself as he raised it, and the higher he raised it, the higher grew the arch of its back, so that he could in no way lift it up. And at last, after he had put forth all his strength, he had been able to do no more than raise one of the cat's paws from the ground.

The lord of Utgard said scoffingly, "That matter has gone as I fancied it would, and Thor is proved to be a very little man beside our youths, that he cannot lift up a cat from the floor.'

Thor was greatly angered, and he cried out, "Now have you made me wrathful with your gibes,[3] and when I am filled with rage, then is my strength increased. Come, let any of you who will, step forth and wrestle with me, and I will show him that my strength is not to be despised."

But no one answered his challenge, and the giants all sat in their places and laughed at him.

"Indeed," said the lord of Utgard, "it appears that there is no one here who would not consider it a disgrace to match himself against one so weak as you have proved yourself to be. But lest you should call us cowards when you tell this tale back home in Asgard, I shall send for Elli, my old nurse, and she will fight with you."

And immediately there came into the hall a tottering old

---

[3] *gibes:* mocking insults

woman. "There stands Elli," laughed the lord of Utgard. "Let us see the great Thor prove himself her equal."

But Thor would not. "Shall I wrestle with a woman, and she an old crone who has seen many years pass by? I, Thor of the Aesir, the strongest of the gods? Why, I should be shamed forevermore that I put forth my strength against a creature so feeble and defenseless."

"She has thrown many a good man before today," said the lord of Utgard. "And if you hold back, all we here shall think that you are afraid of an old woman."

Stung by his taunts, Thor went forward and took hold of the old nurse, but the harder that he gripped her, the firmer she stood; and when, in her turn, she took a grasp of him, he rocked upon his feet. And try as he might, with all his god's strength, Thor was unable to keep his stand, and he fell down upon one knee.

Then the lord of Utgard called to bid the game to cease, and Thor arose, discomforted at his disgrace, that he had been unable to withstand the petty strength of one old woman. But the lord of Utgard said, "Evening is upon us, let us to the feasting, and I warrant that you who are from Asgard will not find our cheer unworthy of your notice." And he led Thor and Loki to seats close by his own; and much of that night they all spent in eating and drinking the good food and ale that were set before them; so that for a while the two gods forgot how they had shown themselves to be of little account in Utgard.

The next day, after the morning meal, Thor and Loki and young Thialfi set off from Utgard early, and the lord of the fortress went a little distance with them to speed them on their way. When they came to the place where they were to part, the lord of Utgard asked Thor with a smile, 'How think you that your journey to Utgard has fallen out? Are you content with it?'

· And Thor frowned and said, 'Truly, I have gained naught but shame and dishonor from my journey to your home.'

But the lord of Utgard shook his head. 'Indeed you have not, great Thor,' he said. 'Now that we have left Utgard many steps behind, I will tell you the truth. If I have the power to keep you out, never again shall you set foot within my fortress. And I will say this also to you, that had I known how great was your strength, I would not have permitted you to enter there even this once. For you must know that it was I whom you met on your way and knew as Skrymir, and I had prepared against your coming to my fortress certain enchantments. The first was when you would have unloosed my sack which held the food. I had fastened it with iron and a spell, so that no one might undo it. And when you struck me those three blows as I slept, the first and least of them would have been enough to kill me, had it reached its mark. But I had put a mountain between myself and you, even that mountain which you see yonder, and your great hammer struck deep into the rock. If you look, you may see how it has cleft it in three places. So also was it sorcery in my fortress. He against whom you, Loki, did contend, my servant Logi, he is wild-fire which can burn the trough and the bones no less easily than it can devour the meat from them. And when you, Thialfi, matched yourself in speed against my Hugi, it could not have been that you should win, for Hugi is thought, and what can run more quickly? And the horn, great Thor, was also an illusion, for when you drank from my horn, though you seemed to have drunk but little, then it was indeed a marvel to us at Utgard, for the other end of the horn was out in the sea, so how could you empty

84

it? When you reach the sea on your journey home, mark well
how the tide-line has dropped lower. And when you tried to lift
up my cat, Thor, that too was a wonder, for it was no cat, but
the Midgard-Serpent, which lies coiled about the earth. When
we saw you raise up one of the cat's paws from the ground, then
did we tremble indeed at your might. And that you should withstand in the wrestling with old Elli, my nurse, and sink no farther
than upon one knee, that was truly marvellous, for she is no other
than old age, and who can resist old age?" After a moment the
lord of Utgard went on, "Now must we part, Thor and red-
haired Loki, and I am glad that it is so. And I may tell you before
we part, that if ever you come again to Utgard, I shall, with all
the wiles and sorcery I know, defend myself and my fortress
against you. Yet I trust that we may never meet again, great
Thor, for you are very mighty."

When Thor heard how he had been tricked, he grasped
Miollnir and flourished it above his head, very wrathful; but in
that instant the lord of Utgard vanished, and was nowhere in
sight. "Let us go back to the fortress and cast it down, stone by
stone," thundered Thor. But when they looked, there before them

85

was the plain whereon had stood the fortress, but Utgard was no longer there, and the wide land was empty.

So Thor and his companions returned the way that they had come, and Thor was very angered; though Loki smiled and shrugged his shoulders, caring little. And when they came to the sea, they saw that it was even as the lord of Utgard had told them, and the waters had diminished with Thor's mighty draughts, and thus were formed the ebb-tides.

Theseus

Young Theseus had a secret. He lived with his mother in a little hut on a wild sea-battered part of the coast called Troezen. For all his poor house and worn-out clothes, he was very proud, for he had a secret: he knew that he was the son of a king. His mother had told him the story one night when their day's catch of fish had been very bad and they were hungry.

"A king, truly," she said. "And one day you will know his name."

"But mother, then why are you not a queen and I a prince? Why don't we live in a palace instead of a hovel?"

"Politics, my son," she said sadly. "All politics . . . You're too young to understand, but your father has a cousin, a very powerful lord with fifty sons. They are waiting for your father to die so they can divide the kingdom. If they knew he had a son of his own to inherit it, they would kill the son immediately."

"When can I go to him? When can I go there and help my father?"

"When you're grown. When you know how to fight your enemies."

This was Theseus' secret . . . and he needed a secret to keep him warm in those long, cold, hard years. One of his worst troubles was his size. His being small for his age bothered him terribly for how could he become a great fighter and help his father against terrible enemies if he couldn't even hold his own against the village boys? He exercised constantly by running up and down the cliffs, swimming in the roughest seas, lifting logs and rocks, bending young trees; and indeed he grew much stronger, but he was still very dissatisfied with himself.

One day, when he had been beaten in a fight with a larger boy, he felt so gloomy that he went down to the beach and lay on the sand watching the waves, hoping that a big one would come along and cover him.

"I will not live this way!" he cried to the wind. "I will not be small and weak and poor. I will be a king, a warrior . . . or I will not be at all."

And then it seemed that the sound of the waves turned to a deep-voiced lullaby, and Theseus fell asleep — not quite asleep, perhaps, because he was watching a great white gull smashing clams open by dropping them on the rocks below. Then the bird swooped down and stood near Theseus' head looking at him, and spoke, "I can crack clams open because they are heavy. Can I do this with shrimps or scallops? No . . . they are too light. Do you know the answer to my riddle?"

"Is it a riddle?"

"A very important one. The answer is this: do not fear your enemy's size, but use it against him. Then his strength will become yours. When you have used this secret, come back, and I will tell you a better one."

Theseus sat up, rubbing his eyes. Was it a dream? Had the gull been there, speaking to him? Could it be? What did it all mean? Theseus thought and thought; then he leaped to his feet and raced down the beach, up the cliff to the village where he found the boy who had just beaten him and slapped him across the face. When the boy, who was almost as big as a man, lunged toward him swinging his big fist, Theseus caught the fist and pulled in the same direction. The boy, swung off balance by his own power, went spinning off his feet and landed headfirst.

"Get up," said Theseus. "I want to try that again."

The big fellow lumbered to his feet and rushed at Theseus, who stooped suddenly. The boy went hurtling over him and landed in the road again. This time he lay still.

"Well," said Theseus, "that was a smart gull."

One by one, Theseus challenged the largest boys of the village; and, by being swift and sure and using their own strength against them, he defeated them all.

Then, he returned to the beach and lay on the sand, watching the waves, and listening as the crashing became a lullaby. Once again, his eyes closed, then opened. The great white seagull was pacing the sand near him.

"Thank you," said Theseus.

"Don't thank me" said the gull. "Thank your father. I am but his messenger."

"My father, the king?"

"King, indeed. But not the king your mother thinks."

"What do you mean?"

"Listen now . . . Your father rules no paltry stretch of earth. His domain is as vast as all the seas, and all that is beneath them, and all that the seas claim. He is the Earthshaker, Poseidon."

"Poseidon . . . my father?"

"You are his son."

"Then why does my mother not know? How can this be?"

"You must understand, boy, that the gods sometimes fall in love with beautiful maidens of the earth, but they cannot appear to the maidens in their own forms. The gods are too large, too bright, too terrifying, so they must disguise themselves. Now, when Poseidon fell in love with your mother, she had just been secretly married to Aegeus, king of Athens. Poseidon disguised himself as her new husband, and you, you are his son. One of many, very many; but he seems to have taken a special fancy to you and plans great and terrible things for you . . . if you have the courage."

"I have the courage," said Theseus. "Let me know his will."

"Tomorrow," said the seagull, "you will receive an unexpected gift. Then you must bid farewell to your mother and go to Athens to visit Aegeus. Do not go by sea. Take the dangerous overland route, and your adventures will begin."

The waves made great crashing music. The wind crooned. A blackness crossed the boy's mind. When he opened his eyes the gull was gone, and the sun was dipping into the sea.

"Undoubtedly a dream," he said to himself. "But the last dream worked. Perhaps this one will too."

The next morning there was a great excitement in the village. A huge stone had appeared in the middle of the road. In this stone was stuck a sword half-way up to its hilt; and a messenger had come from the oracle at Delphi saying that whoever pulled the sword from the stone was a king's son and must go to his father.

When Theseus heard this, he embraced his mother and said, "Farewell."

"Where are you going, my son?"

"To Athens. This is the time we have been waiting for. I shall take the sword from the stone and be on my way."

"But, son, it is sunk so deeply. Do you think you can? Look . . . look . . . the strongest men cannot budge it. There is the smith trying . . . And there the Captain of the Guard . . . And look . . . look at that giant herdsman trying. See how he pulls and grunts. Oh, son, I fear the time is not yet."

"Pardon me," said Theseus, moving through the crowd. "Let me through, please. I should like a turn."

When the villagers heard this, heard the short fragile-looking youth say these words, they exploded in laughter.

"Delighted to amuse you," said Theseus. "Now, watch this."

Theseus grasped the sword by the hilt and drew it from the stone as easily as though he were drawing it from a scabbard; he bowed to the crowd and stuck the sword in his belt. The villagers were too stunned to say anything.

The overland road from Troezen to Athens was the most dangerous in the world. It was infested not only by bandits but also giants, ogres, and sorcerers who lay in wait for travelers and killed them for their money, or their weapons, or just for sport. Those who had to make the trip usually went by boat, preferring the risk of shipwreck and pirates to the terrible mountain brigands. If the trip overland had to be made, travelers banded together, went heavily armed, and kept watch as though on a military march.

Theseus knew all this, but he did not give it a second thought. He was too happy to be on his way . . . leaving his poky little village and his ordinary life. He was off to the great world and adventure. He welcomed the dangers that lay in wait. "The more, the better," he thought. "Where there's danger, there's glory. Why, I shall be disappointed if I am *not* attacked."
He was not to be disappointed.

By nightfall he came to an inn where light was coming from the window, smoke from the chimney. But it was not a cozy sight as the front yard was littered with skulls and other bones.

"They don't do much to attract guests," thought Theseus. "Well . . . I'm tired. It has been a long day. I'd just as soon go to bed now without any more fighting. On the other hand, if an adventure comes my way, I must not avoid it. Let's see what this bone-collector looks like."

He strode to the door and pounded on it, crying, "Land-lord! Landlord, ho!"

The door flew open. In it was framed a greasy-looking giant, resembling Sciron and the pine-bender, but older, filthier, with long, tangled gray hair and a blood-stained gray beard. He had great meaty hands like grappling hooks.

"Do you have a bed for the night?" said Theseus.

"A bed? That I have. Come with me."

He led Theseus to a room where a bed stood — an enormous ugly piece of furniture, hung with leather straps, and chains, and shackles.

"What are all those bolts and bindings for?" said Theseus.

"To keep you in bed until you've had your proper rest."

"Why should I wish to leave the bed?"

"Everyone else seems to. You see, this is a special bed, exactly six feet long from head to foot. And I am a very neat, orderly person. I like things to fit. Now, if the guest is too short for the bed, we attach those chains to his ankles and stretch him. Simple."

"And if he's too long?" said Theseus.

"Oh, well then we just lop off his legs to the proper length."

"I see."

"But don't worry about that part of it. You look like a stretch job to me. Go ahead, lie down."

"And if I do, then you will attach chains to my ankles and stretch me — if I understand you correctly."

"You understand me fine. Lie down."

"But all this stretching sounds uncomfortable."

"You came here. Nobody invited you. Now you've got to take the bad with the good."

"Yes, of course," said Theseus. "I suppose if I decided not to take advantage of your hospitality . . . I suppose you'd *make* me lie down, wouldn't you?"

"Oh, sure. No problem."

"How? Show me."

The inn-keeper, whose name was Procrustes, reached out a great hand, put it on Theseus' chest, and pushed him toward the bed. Theseus took his wrist, and, as the big man pushed, he pulled . . . in the swift shoulder-turning downward snap he had taught himself. Procrustes flew over his shoulder and landed on

the bed. Theseus bolted him fast, took up an ax, and chopped off his legs as they dangled over the footboards. Then, because he did not wish the fellow to suffer, chopped off his head too.

"As you have done by travelers, so are you done by," said Theseus. "You have made your bed, old man. Now lie on it."

He put down the ax, picked up his club, and resumed his journey, deciding to sleep in the open because he found the inn unpleasant.

He went on to Athens. Athens was not yet a great city in those days, but it was far more splendid than any Theseus had seen. He found it quite beautiful with arbors and terraces and marble temples. He suffered from humiliation for, although he was the king's son, his father was in a very weak position so he could not be a real prince.

It was his father's powerful cousin, the tall black-browed Pallas with his fifty fierce sons, who actually ran things. Their estate was much larger and finer than the castle, their private army stronger than the Royal Guard, and Theseus could not bear it.

"Why was I given the sign?" he stormed. "Why did I pull the sword from the stone and come here to Athens? To skulk in the castle like a runaway slave? What difference does it make, Father, how *many* there are? After we fight them, there will be many less. Let's fight! right now!"

"No," said Aegeus, "we cannot. Not yet. It would not be a battle, it would be suicide. They must not know you are here. I am sorry now I had you come all the way to Athens. It is too dangerous. I should have kept you in some little village somewhere, outside of town, where we could have seen each other every day, but where you would not be in such danger."

"Well, if I am no use here, let me go to Crete!" cried Theseus. "If I can't fight our enemies at home, let me try my hand abroad."

"Crete! . . . Oh, my dear boy, no, no . . ," and the old man fell to lamenting for it was in these days that Athens, defeated in a war with Crete, was forced by King Minos to pay a terrible tribute. He demanded that each year the Athenians send him seven of their most beautiful maidens, seven of their strongest young men. These were taken to the Labyrinth and offered to the monster who lived there — the dread Minotaur, half man and half bull — son of Pasiphae and the bull she had fallen in love with. Year after year they were taken from their parents, these seven maidens and seven youths, and were never heard of again. Now the day of tribute was approaching again.

Theseus offered to go himself as one of the seven young men and take his chances with the monster. He kept hammering at his father, kept producing so many arguments, was so electric with impatience and rage, that finally his father consented, and the name Theseus was entered among those who were to be selected for tribute. The night before he left, he embraced Aegeus and said, "Be of good heart, dear sire. I traveled a road that was supposed to be fatal before and came out alive. I met quite a few unpleasant characters on my journey and had a few anxious moments, but I learned from them that the best weapon you can give an enemy is your own fear. So . . . who can tell. I may emerge victorious from the Labyrinth and lead my companions home safely. Then I will be known to the people of Athens and will be able to rouse them against your tyrant cousins and make you a real king."

93

"May the gods protect you, son," said Aegeus. "I shall sacrifice to Zeus and to Ares, and to our own Athene, every day, and pray for your safety."

"Don't forget Poseidon," said Theseus.

"Oh, yes, Poseidon too," said Aegeus. "Now do this for me, son. Each day I shall climb the Hill of the Temple, and from there watch over the sea . . . watching for your ship to return. It will depart wearing black sails, as all the sad ships of tribute do; but if you should overcome the Minotaur, please, I pray you, raise a white sail. This will tell me that you are alive and save a day's vigil."

"That I will do." said Theseus. "Watch for the white sail . . ."

Crete

All Athens was at the pier to see the black-sailed ship depart. The parents of the victims were weeping and tearing their clothing. The maidens and the young men, chosen for their beauty and courage, stood on the deck trying to look proud; but the sound of lamentation reached them, and they wept to see their parents weep. Then Theseus felt the cords of his throat tighten with rage. He stamped his foot on the deck and shouted, "Up anchor, and away!" as though he were the captain of the vessel. The startled crew obeyed, and the ship moved out of the harbor.

Theseus immediately called the others to him. "Listen to me," he said. "You are not to look upon yourselves as victims, or victims you will surely be. The time of tribute has ended. You are to regard this voyage not as a submission but as a military expedition. Everything will change, but first you must change your own way of looking at things. Place your faith in my hands, place yourselves under my command. Will you?"

"We will!" they shouted.

"Good. Now I want every man to instruct every girl in the use of the sword and the battle-ax. We may have to cut our way to freedom. I shall also train you to respond to my signals — whistles, hand-movements — for if we work as a team, we may be able to defeat the Minotaur and confound our enemies."

94

They agreed eagerly. They were too young to live without hope, and Theseus' words filled them with courage. Every day he drilled them, man and maiden alike, as though they were a company of soldiers. He taught them to wrestle in the way he had invented. And this wild young activity, this sparring and fencing, so excited the crew, that they were eager to place themselves under the young man's command.

"Yes," he said. "I will take your pledges. You are Athenians. Right now that means you are poor, defeated, living in fear. But one day 'Athenian' will be the proudest name in the world, a word to make warriors quake in their armor, kings shiver upon their thrones!"

Now Minos of Crete was the most powerful king in all the world. His capital, Knossos, was the gayest, richest, proudest city in the world; and the day, each year, when the victims of the Minotaur arrived from Athens, was always a huge feast-day. People mobbed the streets — warriors with shaven heads and gorgeous feathered cloaks, women in jewels and topless dresses, children, farmers, great swaggering bullherders, lithe bullfighters, dwarfs, peacocks, elephants, and slaves, slaves, slaves from every country known to man. The streets were so jammed no one could walk freely, but the King's Guard kept a lane open from quayside to Palace. And here, each year, the fourteen victims were marched so that the whole city could see them — marched past the crowds to the Palace to be presented to the king to have their beauty approved before giving them to the Minotaur.

On this day of arrival, the excited harbormaster came puffing to the castle, fell on his knees before the throne, and gasped, "Pity, great king, pity . . ."

And then in a voice strangled with fright the harbormaster told the king that one of the intended victims, a young man named Theseus, demanded a private audience with Minos before he would allow the Athenians to disembark.

"My warships!" thundered Minos. "The harbor is full of triremes. Let the ship be seized, and this Theseus and his friends dragged here through the streets."

"It cannot be, your majesty. Their vessel stands over the narrow neck of the harbor. And he swears to scuttle it right there, blocking the harbor, if any of our ships approach."

"Awkward . . . very awkward," murmured Minos. "Quite resourceful for an Athenian, this young man. Worth taking a look at. Let him be brought to me."

Thereupon Theseus was informed that the king agreed to see him privately. He was led to the Palace, looking about eagerly as he was ushered down the lane past the enormous crowd. He had never seen a city like this. It made Athens look like a little fishing village. He was excited and he walked, head high, eyes flashing. When he came to the Palace, he was introduced to the king's daughters, two lovely young princesses, Ariadne and Phaedra.

"I regret that my queen is not here to greet you," said Minos. "But she has become attached to her summer house in the Labyrinth and spends most of her time there."

The princesses were silent, but they never took their eyes off Theseus. He could not decide which one he prefered. Ariadne, he supposed — the other was really still a little girl. But she had a curious cat-faced look about her that intrigued him. However, he could not give much thought to this; his business was with the king.

Finally, Minos signaled the girls to leave the room, and motioned Theseus toward his throne. "You wanted to see me alone," he said. "Here I am. Speak."

"I have a request, your majesty. As the son of my father, Aegeus, King of Athens, and his representative in this court, I ask you formally to stop demanding your yearly tribute."

"Oh, heavens," said Minos. "I thought you would have something original to say. And you come with this threadbare old petition. I have heard it a thousand times and refused it a thousand times."

"I know nothing of what has been done before," said Theseus. "But only of what I must do. You laid this tribute upon Athens to punish the city, to show the world that you were the master. But it serves only to degrade you and show the world that you are a fool."

"Feeding you to the Minotaur is much too pleasant a finale for such an insolent rascal," said Minos. "I shall think of a much more interesting way for you to die — perhaps several ways."

"Let me explain what I mean," said Theseus. "Strange as it seems, I do not hate you. I admire you. You're the most powerful king in the world and I admire power. In fact, I intend to imitate your career. So what I say, I say in all friendliness, and it is this: when you take our young men and women and shut them in the Labyrinth to be devoured by the Minotaur, you are making the whole world forget Minos, the great general Minos, the wise king. What you are forcing upon their attention is Minos, the betrayed husband, the man whose wife disliked him so much she eloped with a bull. And this image of you is what people remember. Drop the tribute, I say, and you will once again live in man's mind as warrior, law-giver, and king."

"You are an agile debater," said Minos, "as well as a very reckless young man, saying these things to me. But there is a flaw in your argument. If I were to drop the tribute, my subjects would construe this as an act of weakness. They would be encouraged to launch conspiracies against me. Other countries under my sway would be encouraged to rebel. It cannot be done."

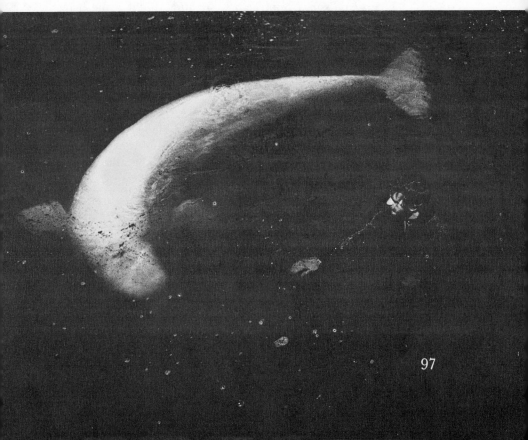

"I can show you a graceful way to let the tribute lapse. One that will not be seen as a sign of weakness. Just tell me how to kill the monster."

"Kill the monster, eh? And return to Athens a hero? And wipe out your enemies there? And then subdue the other cities of Greece until you become leader of a great alliance? And then come visit me again with a huge fleet and an enormous army, and topple old Minos from his throne . . ? Do I describe your ambitions correctly?"

"The future does not concern me," said Theseus. "I take one thing at a time. And the thing that interests me now is killing the Minotaur."

"Oh, forget the Minotaur," said Minos. "How do you know there is one? How do you know it's not some maniac there who ties sticks to his head? Whatever it is, let him rot there in the Labyrinth with his mad mother. I have a better plan for you. My sons are dead. My daughter Ariadne, I notice, looks upon you with favor. Marry her, and become my heir. One day you will rule Crete and Athens both . . . and all the cities of the sea."

"Thank you, sir. I appreciate your offer. But I came here to fight a monster."

"You are mad.

"Perhaps. But this is the only way I know how to be. When I am your age, when the years have thinned my blood, when rage has cooled into judgment, then I will go in for treaties, compromises. Now, I must fight."

"Why is the young fool so confident?" thought Minos to himself. "He acts like a man who knows he is protected by the gods. Can it be true what they say? Is he really the son of Poseidon? Do I have that kind of enemy on my hands? If so, I will make doubly sure to get rid of him."

Then he said aloud, "You are wrong to refuse my offer. I suppose you are made so wildly rash by some old wives' gossip in your little village that you are the son of this god or that. Those mountain villages of yours, they're ridiculous. Every time a child does something out of the way, all the crones and hags get together and whisper, "He's the son of a god, really the son of a god." Is that the way of it? Tell the truth now."

"My truth," said Theseus, "is that I am the son of Poseidon."

"Poseidon, eh? No less. Well, how would you like to prove it?"

"Why should I care to prove it? *I* know. That's enough for me. The whole world has heard that you are the son of Zeus, who courted your mother, Europa, in the guise of a white bull. Everyone has heard this tale; few disbelieve it. But can you prove it?"

"Come with me," said Minos.

He led him out of the Palace, beyond the wall, to a cliff overlooking the sea. He stood tall, raised his arms, and said, "Father Zeus, make me a sign."

Lightning flashed so furiously that the night became brighter than day, and the sky spoke in thunder. Then Minos dropped his arms; the light stopped pulsing in the sky, and the thunder was still.

"Well," said Minos. "Have I proved my parentage?"

"It's an impressive display. I suppose it proves something."

"Then show me you are the son of Poseidon."

Minos took the crown from his head and threw it over the cliff into the sea. They heard the tiny splash far below.

"If you are his son, the sea holds no terror for you. Get me my crown, " said Minos.

Without a moment's hesitation, Theseus stepped to the edge of the cliff and leaped off. As he fell, he murmured, "Father, help me now."

Down he plunged, struck the black water and went under, shearing his way through until he felt his lungs bursting. But he did not kick toward the surface. He let out the air in his chest in a long tortured gasp, and then, breathed in. No strangling rush of water, but a great lungfull of sweet cool air . . . and he felt himself breathing as naturally as a fish. He swam down, down, and as he swam his eyes became accustomed to the color of the night sea; he moved in a deep green light. And the first thing he saw was the crown gleaming on the bottom. He swam down and picked it up.

Theseus stood on the ocean bottom holding the crown in his hand and said, "All thanks, Father Poseidon."

He waited there for the god to answer him, but all he saw were dark gliding shapes, creatures of the sea passing like

shadows. He swam slowly to the surface, climbed the cliff, and walked to where Minos was waiting.

"Your crown, sir."

"Thank you."

"Are you convinced now that Poseidon is my father?"

"I am convinced that the water is more shallow here than I thought. Convinced that you are lucky."

"Luck? Is that not another word for divine favor?"

"Perhaps. At any rate, I am also convinced that you are a dangerous young man. So dangerous that I am forced to strip you of certain advantages allowed those who face the Minotaur. You will carry neither sword nor ax, but only your bare hands . . . And your luck, of course. I think we will not meet again. So farewell." He whistled sharply. His Royal Guard appeared, surrounded Theseus, and marched him off to a stone tower at the edge of the Labyrinth. There they locked him up for the night.

An hour before dawn Ariadne appeared in his cell and said, "I love you, Theseus. I will save you from death if you promise to take me back to Athens with you."

"And how do you propose to save me, lovely princess?"

"Do you know what the Labyrinth is? It is a hedge of a thousand lanes, all leading in, and only one leading out. And this one is so concealed, has so many twists and turns and secret windings that no one can possibly find his way out. Only I can travel the Labyrinth freely. I will lead you in and hide you. I will also lead you around the central chamber where the Minotaur is and lead you out again. You will not even see the monster. Since no one has ever found his way out of the maze, Minos will assume that you have killed the Minotaur, and you will have a chance to get to your ship and escape before the trick is discovered. But you must take me with you."

"It cannot be," said Theseus.

"Don't you believe me? It's all true. Look . . ."

She took from her tunic a ball of yellow silk thread and dropped it on the floor. The ball swiftly rolled across the room, unwinding itself as it went. It rolled around the bench, wrapped itself around one of Theseus' ankles, rolled up the wall, across the ceiling and down again. Then Ariadne tugged sharply on her end of the thread, and the ball reversed itself, rolling back the way it had come, reeling in its thread as it rolled. Back to Ariadne it rolled and leaped into her hand.

"This was made for me by old Daedalus," said Ariadne. "It was he who built the Labyrinth, you know. And my father shut him up in it too. I used to go visit him there. He made me this magic ball of thread so that I would always be able to find my way to him, and find my way back. He was very fond of me."

"I'm getting very fond of you too," said Theseus.

"Do you agree?" cried Ariadne. "Will you let me guide you in the Labyrinth and teach you how to avoid the monster, and fool my father. Say you will. Please . . ."

"I'll let you guide me through the maze," said Theseus. "Right to where the monster dwells. You can stay there and watch the fight. And when it's over, you can lead me back."

"No, no, I won't be able to. You'll be dead! It's impossible for you to fight the Minotaur."

"It is impossible for me not to."

"You won't even be armed."

"I have always traveled light, sweet princess, and taken

my weapons from the enemy. I see no reason to change my habits now. Are you the kind of girl who seeks to change a man's habits? If you are, I don't think I will take you back to Athens."

"Oh, please, do not deny me your love," she said. "I will do as you say."

The next morning when the Royal Guard led Theseus out of the tower and forced him into the outer lane of the Labyrinth, Ariadne was around the first bend, waiting. She tied one end of the thread to a branch of the hedge, then dropped the ball to the ground. It rolled slowly, unwinding; they followed, hand in hand. It was pleasant, walking in the Labyrinth. The hedge grew tall above their heads and was heavy with little white sweet-smelling flowers. The lane turned and twisted and turned again, but the ball of thread ran ahead, and they followed it. Theseus heard a howling.

"Sounds like the wind," he said.

"No, it is not the wind. It is my mad mother, howling."

They walked farther. They heard a rumbling, crashing sound.

"What's that?"

"That is my brother. He's hungry."

They continued to follow the ball of thread. Now the hedges grew so tall the branches met above their heads, and it was dark. Ariadne looked up at him, sadly. He bent his head and brushed her lips in a kiss.

"Please don't go to him," she said. "Let me lead you out now. He will kill you. He has the strength of a bull and the cunning of a man."

"Who knows?" said Theseus. "Perhaps he has the weakness of a man and the stupidity of a bull." He put his hand over her mouth. "Anyway, let me think so because I must fight him, you see, and I'd rather not frighten myself beforehand."

The horrid roaring grew louder and louder. The ball of thread ran ahead, ran out of the lane, into an open space. And here, in a kind of meadow surrounded by the tall hedges of the Labyrinth, stood the Minotaur.

Theseus could not believe his eyes. The thing was more fearsome than in his worst dreams. What he had expected was a bull's head on a man's body. What he saw was something about ten feet tall shaped like a man, like an incredibly huge and brutally muscular man, but covered with a short dense brown fur. It had a man's face, but a squashed, bestialized one, with poisonous red eyes, great blunt teeth, and thin leathery lips. Sprouting out of its head were two long heavy polished horns. Its feet were hooves, razor sharp; its hands were shaped like a man's hands, but much larger and hard as horn. When it clenched them they were great fists of bone.

It stood pawing the grass with a hoof, peering at Theseus with its little red eyes. There was a bloody slaver on its lips.

Now, for the first time in all his battles, Theseus became unsure of himself. He was confused by the appearance of the monster. It filled him with a kind of horror that was beyond fear, as if he were wrestling a giant spider. So when the monster lowered its head and charged, thrusting those great bone lances at him, Theseus could not move out of the way.

There was only one thing to do. Drawing himself up on tiptoe, making himself as narrow as possible, he leaped into the air and seized the monster's horns. Swinging himself between the horns, he somersaulted onto the Minotaur's head, where he crouched, gripping the horns with desperate strength. The monster bellowed with rage and shook its head violently. But Theseus held on. He thought his teeth would shake out of his head; he felt his eyeballs rattling in their sockets. But he held on.

Now, if it can be done without one's being gored, somersaulting between the horns is an excellent tactic when fighting a real bull; but the Minotaur was not a real bull; it had hands. So when Theseus refused to be shaken off but stood on the head between the horns trying to dig his heels into the beast's eyes, the Minotaur stopped shaking his head, closed his great horny fist, big as a cabbage and hard as a rock, and struck a vicious backward blow, smashing his fist down on his head, trying to squash Theseus as you squash a beetle.

This is what Theseus was waiting for. As soon as the fist swung toward him, he jumped off the Minotaur's head, and the fist smashed between the horns, full on the skull. The Minotaur's knees bent, he staggered and fell over; he had stunned himself. Theseus knew he had only a few seconds before the beast would recover his strength. He rushed to the monster,

took a horn in both hands, put his foot against the ugly face, and putting all his strength in a sudden tug, broke the horn off at the base. He leaped away. Now he, too, was armed, and with a weapon taken from the enemy.

The pain of the breaking horn goaded the Minotaur out of his momentary swoon. He scrambled to his feet, uttered a great choked bellow, and charged toward Theseus, trying to hook him with his single horn. Bone cracked against bone as Theseus parried with his horn. It was like a duel now, the beast thrusting with his horn, Theseus parrying, thrusting in return. Since the Minotaur was much stronger, it forced Theseus back — back until it had Theseus pinned against the hedge. As soon as he felt the first touch of the hedge, Theseus disengaged, ducked past the Minotaur, and raced to the center of the meadow, where he stood, poised, arm drawn back. For the long pointed horn made as good a javelin as it did a sword, and so could be used at a safer distance.

The Minotaur whirled and charged again. Theseus waited until he was ten paces away, and then whipped his arm forward, hurling the javelin with all his strength. It entered the bull's neck and came out the other side. But so powerful was the Minotaur's rush, so stubborn his bestial strength, that he trampled on with the sharp horn through his neck and ran right over Theseus, knocking him violently to the ground. Then it whirled to try to stab Theseus with its horn, but the blood was spouting fast now, and the monster staggered and fell on the ground beside Theseus.

Ariadne ran to the fallen youth. She turned him over, raised him in her arms; he was breathing. She kissed him. He opened his eyes, looked around and saw the dead Minotaur; then he looked back at her and smiled. He climbed to his feet, leaning heavily on Ariadne.

"Tell your thread to wind itself up again, Princess. We're off for Athens."

When Theseus came out of the Labyrinth there was an enormous crowd of Cretans gathered. They had heard the sound of fighting, and, as the custom was, had gathered to learn of the death of the hostages. When they saw the young man covered with dirt and blood, carrying a broken horn, with Ariadne clinging to his arm, they raised a great shout.

Minos was there, standing with his arms folded. Phaedra was at his side. Theseus bowed to him and said, "Your majesty, I have the honor to report that I have rid your kingdom of a foul monster."

"Prince Theseus," said Minos. "According to the terms of the agreement, I must release you and your fellow hostages."

"Your daughter helped me, king. I have promised to take her with me. Have you any objection?"

"I fancy it is too late for objections. The women of our family haven't had much luck in these matters. Try not to be too beastly to her."

"Father," said Phaedra, "she will be lonesome there in far-off Athens. May I not go with her and keep her company?"

"You too?" said Minos. He turned to Theseus. "Truly, young man, whether or not Poseidon has been working for you, Aphrodite surely has."

"I will take good care of your daughters, king," said Theseus. "Farewell."

And so, attended by the Royal Guard, Theseus, his thirteen happy companions, and the two Cretan princesses, walked through the mobbed streets from the Palace to the harbor. There they boarded their ship.

It was a joyous ship that sailed northward from Crete to Athens. There was feasting and dancing night and day. And every young man aboard felt himself a hero too, and every maiden a princess. And Theseus was lord of them all, drunk with strength and joy. He was so happy he forgot his promise to his father — forgot to tell the crew to take down the black sail and raise a white one.

King Aegeus, keeping a lonely watch on the hill of the Temple, saw first a tiny speck on the horizon. He watched it for a long time and saw it grow big and then bigger. He could not tell whether the sail was white or black; but as it came nearer, his heart grew heavy. The sail seemed to be dark. The ship came nearer, and he saw that it wore a black sail. He knew that his son was dead.

"I have killed him," he cried. "In my weakness, I sent him off to be killed. I am unfit to be king, unfit to live. I must go to Tartarus immediately and beg his pardon there."

And the old king leaped from the hill, dived through the steep air into the sea far below, and was drowned. He gave that lovely blue, fatal stretch of water its name for all time — the Aegean Sea.

Theseus, upon his return to Athens, was hailed as king. The people worshipped him. He swiftly raised an army, wiped out his powerful cousins, and then led the Athenians forth into many battles, binding all the cities of Greece together in an alliance. Then, one day he returned to Crete to reclaim the crown of Minos which once he had recovered from the sea.

Further Reading

Black Folktales, *by Julius Lester.*

The Children of Odin; The Book of Northern Myths,
by Padraic Colum.

Once Upon A Totem, *by Christie Harris.*

The Stars In Our Heaven: Myths and Fables, *by Peter Lum.*

Tales of the Norse Gods and Heroes, *by Barbara Leonie Picard.*

Tales The Muses Told, *by Roger Lancelyn Green.*

Thunder of the Gods, *by Dorothy Hosford.*

A Wonder Book and Tanglewood Tales,
by *Nathaniel Hawthorne.*

Words From The Myths, *by Isaac Asimov.*

The World of Manabozho; Tales of the Chippewa Indians.
by Thomas Leekley.

Next, see "Myth Making," "Tall Tales," "A Hero or Heroine for Our Times," "Hell and Heaven," "Mod Myths and Legends," "Want Ad Puzzles," and "Picture Symbols" in MAKING THINGS UP; "Reading to Others" in PROJECTS AND PROCESSES and "Story in Disguise" and "Story Over" in ACTING OUT.

Stories on circled pages have been recorded. Look for them under *Myths* in the LISTENING LIBRARY.